CW01494520

SACK

the

ECONOMISTS

AND DISBAND
THEIR
DEPARTMENTS

Geoff Davies

The disastrous flaws in mainstream economics,
and how economies can serve our total wellbeing

First published in 2013 by BWM Books Pty Ltd
Canberra, Australia

ISBN 978-0-9923603-6-8

1. Economics

Davies, Geoffrey Frederick, 1944-

Praise for Sack the Economists

This book raises many interesting questions, most importantly, why does anyone take economists seriously when it comes to discussing the economy?

– Dean Baker,
Co-Director, Center for Economic and Policy Research,
Washington D.C.

Geoff Davies has a very good idea. Economics has locked itself into an intellectual cul-de-sac. Even its failure to anticipate the global economic crisis was not enough to force it out. So let's sack the economists and let real scientists take over this vital but currently dangerous discipline.

– Steve Keen,
Economist and author of the popular book
Debunking Economics.

With delightful wit and insightful analogies, geophysicist Geoff Davies dissects the inconsistencies — and the inanities — of mainstream economics. Don't blame Adam Smith, he makes clear, for the mess this mainstream has become. Blame the intellectually lazy and morally obtuse careerists who practice an economics that in no way, shape, or form resembles the science they claim it to be. In the end, *Sack the Economists* helps us understand, plutocracy never works — and neither does an economics that refuses to discomfort our plutocrats.

– Sam Pizzigati,
Institute for Policy Studies, Washington, D.C.,
and author of *The Rich Don't Always Win*.

Praise for Geoff Davies

If change is going to come, it will be from other professions, like physics, engineering and biology, who are used to modelling the dynamic, unstable real world rather than fantasies of equilibrium. They should be emboldened by this crisis to step onto the turf of economics and take the field over from the economists. **Geoff Davies was one of the very first** to do this, long before the current crisis hit, and **his physics- and biology-inspired work is part of the promise of a future economics** that is actually useful–unlike the downright dangerous fantasies of today's neoclassical economists."

– Economist **Steve Keen,**
author of *Debunking Economics*.

Praise for Economia

Geoff Davies turns his critical scientific gaze on contemporary economic orthodoxy and finds it deeply deficient. His work makes a strong case for a radical reconstruction of economic arrangements if we are to live more fruitfully and harmoniously.

– Frank Stilwell,
Professor of Political Economy, University of Sydney.

Imagine a much more equal and inclusive society than we have now. It has old-fashioned family values, solid local communities, and full employment in an efficient and sustainable market economy with a debt-free money supply and no executive plunder. Impossible? Perhaps. But Geoff Davies' project is distinguished by such common sense, hard science, practicality, surprise, fine writing and expert contempt for orthodox economics, it's a joy to read for visionaries and sceptics alike.

– **Hugh Stretton,**
author of *Economics, A New Introduction*

For all its apparent logic and orderliness neoliberal economics is also deeply irrational, as Geoff Davies lucidly illustrates in his immensely readable *Economia* ... Davies, like many others is turning to an ecological model to explain our economic behaviour and its impact on the quality of our lives and on the planet.

– **Keith Gallasch,**
RealTime magazine, June/July 2004: The arts, ecologically.
Full article.

... one of the best analyses of the sustainability problem that I have so far encountered... The reader is taken on a journey of discovery that revolves around an excellent critique of economics, counterpoised against truly amazing insights into how all of life has self-organised from the simple origins of life through to the current complexity of the biosphere. ... its lucid analysis from a systems perspective provides an excellent insight to ...the often overlooked systemic role of the current financial system in driving unsustainability.

– Richard Sanders,
CSIRO Sustainability Network Update 41E
(pdf download, 464 kb).
Full review

Everyone now knows that economics is a pseudo-science and that economists, in the words of the late Alistair Cooke, are "varieties of necromancers". Still, there are few books that set out clearly why modern economic theory is humbug. This remarkable book — which systematically pillories modern economic concepts, from globalism to laissez-faire economics — has been written by a senior fellow at the Australian National University whose field of expertise is geophysics. A geophysicist writing about economics? Well, better than an economist writing about economics. If you are depressed whenever you hear an economic argument that common sense tells you is rubbish, then this is the book for you. Davies dissects modern economics and intelligently argues that it is possible to create a new economic system that will benefit society. This may be utopia, but it is utopia beautifully argued.

– Bruce Elder,
Sydney Morning Herald Weekend Edition, April 24-25, 2004.

Davies has been very successful in bringing a wide range of related ideas together in an engaging and persuasive way. In addition his Part 7, Malign Money, provides a lucid explanation – which I have not seen elsewhere – of how the form of money supply chosen influences economic behaviour and social development – and of the damage caused by the neo-classical choice of monetary mechanisms.

– Change Management Monitor.
Full review here; commentary comparing and contrasting *Economia* with Fritjof Capra's *The Hidden Connections* download (pdf, 88 kb).

… wonderfully readable and easily the most inspiring critique I have seen of the legalised robbery which passes for economic productivity these days.

– Brian Jenkins,
Citizen's Voice, June 2004. Full review.

I find Davies' arguments refreshing and convincing. They cannot be ignored. … if Davies is even half right, we, the people, must urgently modify the economic model which drives all of our financial institutions, nearly all of our current politicians and all of our public services.

– Bob Douglas,
Emeritus Professor, Australian National University, and Chair of the Board of Australia21, reviewing in *The Canberra Times* 13 March, 2004. Download the full review (pdf, 620 kb).

Praise for The Nature of the Beast

In *The Nature of the Beast* Geoff Davies makes a valuable contribution to the public debate about the big issues facing humanity today. As that great Australian, Dr. Nugget Coombs, wrote after decades of esteemed public service:

"There is nothing divinely ordained about the economic system: it is the product of human ingenuity … and can therefore properly be questioned, criticised and, if a better alternative exists, rejected."

Not many Australians have taken up this challenge. Geoff has. He raises important questions and criticisms of our present way of doing things, and offers pointers to a better economic system and a better human society. I admire that he sees the environment as having a central place in the design of a viable and sustainable alternative and that he displays an underlying faith in the capacity of people ultimately to think and act for the good of all.

– The Honourable
Tom Uren, **AO,** former Australian Federal Labor Minister:

In *The Nature of the Beast* Geoff Davies is much more in command of the material, and his text is highly readable and clear even for people who are not well informed about economics. … he makes an excellent effort to explain what's wrong with the present way we think about economics and how we could easily change that to our great advantage. **Essential reading.**

– John Stephen
Veitch of Open Future, NZ:

CONTENTS

1

ECONOMISTS DON'T KNOW WHAT THEY'RE TALKING ABOUT

The walking dead

IN 1994 Paul Ormerod published a book called *The Death of Economics*[1]. He argued economists don't know what they're talking about. In 2001 Steve Keen published a book called *Debunking Economics: the naked emperor of the social sciences*[2], with a second edition in 2011 subtitled *The naked emperor dethroned?*[3]. Keen also argued economists don't know what they're talking about.

Neither of these books, nor quite a few others, has had the desired effect. Mainstream economics has sailed serenely on its way, declaiming, advising, berating, sternly lecturing, deciding, teaching, pontificating. Meanwhile half of Europe and many regions and groups in the United States are in depression, and fascism is making a comeback. The last big depression spawned Hitler. This one is promoting Golden Dawn in Greece and similar extremist movements elsewhere. In the anglophone world a fundamentalist right-wing ideology is enforcing an increasingly narrow political correctness centred on "free" markets and the right of the rich to do and say whatever they like. "Freedom", but only for some, and without responsibility.

Evidently Ormerod and Keen were too subtle. It's true their books also get a bit technical at times, especially Keen's, but then they were addressing the profession, trying to bring it to its senses, to reform it from the inside. That seems to have been their other mistake. They produced example after example of how mainstream ideas fail, but still they had no effect. I think the message was addressed to the wrong audience, and was just too subtle. Economics is naked and dead, but never mind the stink, just prop up the corpse and carry on.

Oh, but look! The corpse is moving. It's getting up and walking. Time to call in John Quiggin, author of *Zombie Economics: how dead ideas still walk among us*[4]. Perhaps he'll show us how to shoot it in the head, or whatever it takes to finally stop a zombie.

Well, I think it's clear we can't be too subtle. We need to speak in plain English, to everyone, and get straight to the point. Economists don't know what they're talking about. We should remove economists from positions of power and influence. Get them out of treasuries, central banks, media, universities, where ever they spread their baleful ignorance.

Economists don't know how businesses work, they don't know how financial markets work, they can't begin to do elementary accounting, they don't know where money comes from nor how banks work, they think private debt has no effect on the economy, their favourite theory is a laughably irrelevant abstraction and they never learnt that mathematics on its own is not science. They ignore well-known evidence that clearly contradicts their theories.

Other academics should look into this discipline called economics that lurks in their midst. Practitioners of proper academic rigour, like historians, ecologists, physicists, psychologists, systems scientists, engineers, even lawyers, will be shocked. Academic economics is an incoherent grab bag of mathematical abstraction, assertion, failure to heed observations, misrepresentation of history and sources, rationalisation of archaic money-lending practices, and wishful thinking. It missed the computational boat that liberated other fields from old analytical mathematics and overly-restrictive assumptions. It is ignorant of major fields of modern knowledge in biology, ecology, psychology, anthropology, physics and systems science.

Though many economists themselves may not realise it, economics is an ideology rationalised by a dog's breakfast of superficial arguments and defended by dense thickets of jargon and arcane mathematics. The ideology is an old one: the rich and powerful know best, the rest of us are here to serve them.

The latest guise of this ideology is called neoliberalism (and also known as economic rationalism, market fundamentalism, Thatcherism, Reaganism and neoconservatism). It espouses "free" markets and minimal government: just the ticket for the rich and powerful to do what they want. "Freedom", in this world view, does not really mean freedom, it means freedom of the rich from restraints imposed by the rest of us, usually through government. It means freedom to manipulate markets, the media and society for the benefit of a minority. It severely constrains the freedom of most of us. Neoliberalism is the sun-worship of the modern Pharaohs.

These claims may be a little controversial. While many will instantly recognise truths from their own experience, others might say yes, but not *all* economists are so ignorant. Well, it's true I have overstated the case. Only *most* economists are so ignorant. So I'll refer to *mainstream economics,* to distinguish it from various marginalised schools of thought and individuals, some of whom do actually have something useful to say about how economies work. For the *in* crowd, I'm talking about neoclassical economics, the economics built around the abstract neoclassical theory, the one that predicts economies are usually close to equilibrium and market crashes are impossible.

However everything I have said is true about mainstream, neoclassical economics. It is pseudo-science, and its adherents have no idea how economies work. That is why they allowed the US sub-prime mortgage bubble to blow up and burst, precipitating the Global Financial Crisis, and why they are making things much worse with austerity policies. Plenty of people saw the Global Financial Crisis coming, and warned about it, and plenty of people are now pointing out how austerity only makes things worse. But mainstream economists are blinded by irrelevant concepts and gross ignorance, and can see none of this.

I do not mean to malign economists personally, they are undoubtedly genuine people wanting to improve the world. However they have been sorely misled. They have been pumped full of equations and required to master difficult mathematical manipulations. This has left them and their professors little time to critically examine assumptions, history, relevant observations, other fields of knowledge and alternative possibilities. Most will have moved into a busy job and never had much chance to reflect on such things. However the profession collectively, and its leaders, are guilty of intellectual laziness, at best, and more plausibly of hubris. University professors are supposed to be continually renovating their field, bringing in new knowledge and new approaches, identifying inadequacies, finding more useful conceptions.

If you think I am being a bit harsh, I am not alone in this judgement. Here is a relatively "respectable" economist (meaning he was able to get at least a good second-rank academic job, at the University of Texas, in spite of his views). His name is James Galbraith[5], and yes he is the son of the famous iconoclastic Harvard economist John Kenneth Galbraith.

> Leading active members of today's economics profession... have formed themselves into a kind of Politburo for correct economic thinking. As a general rule – as one might generally expect from a gentleman's club – this has placed them on the wrong side of every important policy issue, and not just recently but for decades. They predict disaster where none occurs. They deny the possibility of events that then happen. ... They oppose the most basic, decent and sensible reforms, while offering placebos instead. They are always surprised when something untoward (like a recession) actually occurs. And when finally they sense that some position cannot be sustained, they do not re-examine their ideas. They do not consider the possibility of a flaw in logic or theory. Rather, they simply change the subject. No one loses face, in this club, for having been wrong. No one is dis-invited from presenting papers at later annual meetings. And still less is anyone from the outside invited in.

This remains the essential problem. As I have documented – and only in part – there is a rich and promising body of economics – theory and evidence – entirely suited to the study of financial crisis and its enormous problems. This work is significant in ways in which the entire corpus of mainstream economics – and including recent fashions like the new "behavioral economics" – is not. And it brings great clarity to thinking about the implications of the Great Crisis through which we are still passing today. But where is it, inside the economics profession? Essentially, nowhere.

It is therefore pointless to continue with conversations centered on the conventional economics, futile to keep on arguing with Tweedledum and Tweedledee. The urgent need is instead to expand the academic space and the public visibility of ongoing work that is of actual value when faced with the many deep problems of economic life in our time. The urgent task is to make possible careers in those areas, and for people with those perspectives, that have been proven worthy by events. The followers of John Kenneth Galbraith, of Hyman Minsky and of Wynne Godley can claim this distinction. The task now is to increase their numbers and to reward their work.

There have been severe critics of mainstream economics for a very long time. Steve Keen[3] cites in particular Piero Sraffa[6] writing in 1926, John Meynard Keynes[7] writing in 1936, and Hyman Minsky[8] writing in 1977, but he also recites the names Blatt, Garengani, Goodwin, Kalecky, Kaldor, and Veblen "to name a few". These people were not just criticising aspects of economics, they were saying that the central theory of free markets, which is known as the neoclassical theory, was wrong.

6

More recently, here is US economist and commentator Dean Baker[9], co-winner of the Revere Award of the World Economics Association and co-director of the Center for Economic and Policy Research in Washington DC:

> The news that the UK, with negative growth in the fourth quarter of 2012, faces the prospect of a triple-dip recession, should be the final blow to the intellectual credibility of deficit hawks. You just can't get more wrong than this flat-earth bunch of economic policy-makers.
>
> They're pretty much batting zero. They failed to foresee the collapse of housing bubbles in the US and Europe and its consequent downturn. They grossly underestimated its severity after it hit. And their policy prescription of austerity has been shown to be wrong everywhere that applied it: in the US, the eurozone and, especially, the UK.
>
> By all rights, these folks should be laughed out of town. They should be retrained for a job more suited to their skill set – preferably, something that doesn't involve numbers, or people.

So most economists should be retrained for a job more suited to their skill set. (But not for poetry, or we might end up with more Vogon poetry, the third-worst poetry in the universe. On reflection, poetry relates to people and their perceptions, so economists can be ruled out of that profession too.) If any economists can demonstrate that their favourite theory bears some passing resemblance to the real world, they should be allowed to apply for another job using some of their present skills, but not as an *economist,* nor in an *economics* department.

Economies are not separate from societies, much less dominant over societies. Economies are the way societies make their living. If there is any pretence of democracy, then a society can choose to be however it wishes, and the economy would

7

then, sensibly, be tailored to support that kind of society. So an economy is a subordinate part of a society. In a functioning biosphere, a human society is in turn subordinate to the biosphere, at least if it desires its descendants to be around for anything like as long as its ancestors.

Therefore the term *economics* needs to be superseded by something more expansive. The old-fashioned term *political economy* at least allows that human society is involved, if we generously interpret politics as the means by which we arrive at collective decisions. So Departments of Political Economy could be allowable, at least until we arrive at a more concise title than the Department of People, Societies, the Ways They Make Their Livings and Their Relationships With the Rest of the Living World.

A possibly appropriate term might be *socionomy*. It already sounds like a combination of sociology and economy. It might also suggest including the more material and quantitative aspects of society, with no disrespect to sociology intended. Later in this book you will encounter the term *sociocracy*, a more intrinsically social way of governing, so together they might allow room for new conceptions of how our societies work. But what about the rest of the living world? *Ecosocionomy? Biosocionomy?* I'll leave it so someone more inspired.

Staying with political economy for the moment, the less benighted ex-economists might then apply to be Political Economists. Many of them would still fall at the second hurdle, due to the culture shock of encountering scholarly integrity, whereupon they too would be consigned to the communes and salt mines. Those few economists who made it into a new department would be stimulated and guided by their encounters with academics from other fields, who would bring knowledge, creativity and rigour.

Better ideas

A modest amount of investigation, using readily available observations and some modern ideas to make sense of them, readily shows there is no basis in theory or practice for the claim that free markets are the best possible way to organise an economy. That is the central tenet of neoliberal ideology, and it has dominated the world for the past several decades. So neoliberalism is wrong, and the fact the world is in a big mess is not a surprise.

The same investigation reveals that central planning of economies will not work either. Economies are much too nimble, lively, dynamic for that. Economies are more like living systems than clockwork mechanisms, which ought not to be a surprise since at least some components of economies – people – are living, social beings, as distinct from the calculating reptiles[10] mainstream economists assume us to be. So an exclusively socialist economy is not much good either, as the Soviet Union and China found out.

Further investigation, using modern systems concepts with a dash of ancient wisdom, suggests economies, and living things, do not thrive if they are based exclusively on competition, to the exclusion of cooperation. Neither do they thrive if they are based exclusively on cooperation, to the exclusion of competition. That disposes of the two great twentieth-century ideologies. Neither old capitalism nor old socialism is any good, so we ought to give up fighting wars over them.

A bit of reflection will reveal that *both* competition and cooperation are important – in our daily lives, in our families and in any community. A healthy life balances our personal needs, and the expression of our uniqueness, with the needs of our family, community and society. That is normal.

9

The neoliberal reliance exclusively on competition is an unhealthy aberration, just as much as the communist reliance exclusively on cooperation was an unhealthy aberration.

This line of thinking leads us towards a potentially much more productive way of thinking about economies. A herd of wild horses is potentially very powerful, but only if they can be tamed, harnessed and sensibly guided will they become useful to us. Similarly, markets are clearly powerful, but they need to be understood, harnessed and guided if they are to do beneficial work for us. Markets can be guided by managing the incentives under which they operate, with some regulation of obviously harmful behaviour.

If we rid ourselves of the ridiculous concepts currently imposed on our economies, there is a far healthier kind of economy waiting for us to try, and to learn its ways, neither socialism nor capitalism but transcending both. The mixed, social democratic economies of the post-war decades are the nearest approximation so far to what is possible. The period roughly from 1950 to 1970 saw the greatest gain in wealth of the greatest number (in the "developed countries") of any modern period. GDP growth was high, unemployment was ridiculously low by current standards (averaging only 1.3% in Australia and around 3% in the OECD) and inflation was low. This was true even though governments involved themselves quite a lot in the economy.

For all the hype over the past few decades about freeing up markets, deregulating, privatising and all the rest, the resulting performance never matched the performance of those post-war decades. GDP growth was slower and unemployment was much higher. Median wages in the United States have hardly changed for thirty years, and inequality everywhere increased. Then came the big crash of the GFC, which ought to have totally discredited market-fundamentalists, but the evidence was already strong that freed markets were not working as well as the managed markets of the post-war decades.

However we can do better than social democracy, better than an uneasy truce between opposing ideologies based on simplistic views of human nature. Instead we can embrace as natural and healthy our innately opposing tendencies to cooperate and to compete, and learn to balance them in productive ways. That balancing is what makes life unpredictable, and rich.

The resulting economies could also be made compatible with the natural living world, which is good because at present we are rapidly ruining the world that is our total and exclusive life support system. It would be possible, in other words, to live well while respecting others and having the natural world thrive around us.

Promoting debate

In my experience even those economists who dissent most strongly from the mainstream still do not agree with all the criticisms I make, nor all the reforms I advocate here. I think that is mainly because we have very different perspectives. Anyone with any training in economics has to find their way out of the morass, and it tends to be difficult to "unlearn" things that have become familiar mental furniture. There is also a lot of agonising among "heterodox" economists about methodology and philosophy, symptomatic of a lack of experience with a real scientific approach. On the other hand I am an experienced scientist finding my way in from the outside. I might miss some things, time will be the judge of that, but perhaps I more readily recognise things that are unjustified, or I am more willing to name them and face the implications.

11

Perhaps I bring a broader perspective as well, and as a result focus on more than one problem. There are economists who agree more or less with each of the criticisms I make here. There are just none I can think of who would feature all of the problems highlighted here. Neither am I aware of any economist who straightforwardly draws out the fundamental implications of identifying economies as *complex systems* (Chapter 3) nor who argues for separating the supply of money from investment, thereby removing perhaps the strongest destabiliser of our highly unstable economies (Chapter 9).

Anyway I don't see such differences among the dissenters as a problem. My main objective here is to break down the wall of silence that insulates the mainstream from criticism. If the subject is opened up, then we can sensibly debate our differences.

2

BOOM CRASH OPERA

THE Global Financial Crisis of 2007-8 became what is variously known as the Great Recession or the Second Great Depression, which still has much of the world in its grip. It is widely acknowledged to be the worst economic malfunction since the Great Depression of 1928-39. It is also notable because of the almost complete failure of the mainstream economics profession to anticipate it, let alone to adopt policies that would mitigate it or prevent it from happening at all.

Forever blowing bubbles

The Great Recession and the Great Depression are far from the only two such malfunctions. There was a severe depression in the 1890s and other booms and crashes stretching back through centuries at least to the Dutch tulip mania of the 1630s. More recently there have been the stock market crash of 1987, the Asian currency meltdown of 1998, the dot-com bubble of 2001, and national crises in Mexico, Russia, Argentina and Brazil. Because such crashes cause such disruption and misery, it is important to understand why they happen.

The GFC is a useful example because its cause can be seen more clearly than some. The GFC was triggered by the collapse of an excessive build-up of mortgage debt, in the United States in particular. In a nutshell, banks profit from making loans, loans allow people to bid up the price of housing, and higher housing prices are used as collateral for bigger loans. Eventually the loan repayments become too large for some people to afford, they default, prices start to fall, more people default, prices go into free fall, many people lose money, and many people lose their homes.

Usually a rising price spiral like that requires speculation to drive it to excess. If house prices continue to rise, speculators buy houses in the expectation they will be able to sell them later for a windfall profit. The speculation pushes prices higher still, hence the term *speculative bubble*. In the US there were other practices that blew the bubble to greater extremes than ever before. I'll come back to those later.

The inflation and bursting of a speculative bubble is a signature of a market failure. Markets are supposed to send feedback signals that correct prices and pull them back to an optimum level before they deviate too far above, or below. A rising number of defaults should signal to the bank not to use rising housing prices as collateral for bigger loans. People would not then be able to bid the prices up further. However the greed of speculators blocks out that signal and allows prices to rise even higher. Thus we already have reason to question the zeal of market fundamentalists, who claim free markets almost always work and almost always are best.

This account also raises another important question that seems hardly ever to be asked. Why does the failure of some people's investments, or some people's gambles, cause such widespread disruption? If a gambler loses his money on the horses, he and his family suffer, but his money has just been transferred to the bookmaker who is free to spend it, so the economy as a whole is not much affected. If the mythical capitalist invests his savings in a new widget factory, but nobody wants widgets and he goes broke, then the capitalist and his family suffer, but the factory builders will have spent his money and the larger economy will be not much changed.

So, why does the failure of investments in a market crash disrupt everyone else's routine business? In US vernacular, why does a crash on Wall Street cause such havoc on Main Street?

The reason, in essence, is that when you get a mortgage loan, the loan money that appears in your bank account is mostly new money, created out of nothing. The "loan" is not a loan of other people's savings. Instead, only ten percent or less of the loan comes from other people's savings and deposits, and the rest is created by a few strokes of a keyboard. Let there be $90,000 dollars, and let it come to rest in Joe Bloggs' loan account. This fact is well known to bankers, and even to economists. If you search for "fractional reserve banking" you can read about it, though it probably won't be explained as simply as I just did. It's also a little tricky following the implications through several cycles of loan and subsequent deposit, and one good explanation is in a textbook by Heilbroner and Thurow[11]. You may also read that bank loans these days are more complicated than the classic fractional reserve system, but that doesn't change the essence of the argument here.

15

There are several really important implications of this way of making loans. For the moment I'll just focus on one. A new loan increases the total amount of money in the economy. It increases the total purchasing power available in the economy. Conversely, as the loan is paid back the amount of money and purchasing power decrease.

If loans are being issued and paid back at a steady rate, then the total purchasing power in the economy will be steady. However if the number or value of loans is increasing, then so will total purchasing power. If you borrow money to have a new house built, then your builder gets some of that money, and he can go and buy a new TV. The new money flows on through other transactions, and the economy is thereby "stimulated". If the total value of loans is increasing, then more money is being added to the economy and more people have more money to spend. Times are good.

On the other hand if you find you are overstretched and having trouble making your loan payments, then you may have to cut back on other spending – keep the old car going for a while longer, don't eat out as much. If lots of people are cutting back like you, then spending slows, and the economy goes off the boil. Times are not so good.

In the US mortgage bubble, the number and value of loans kept increasing for a long time. Lots of new money flowed into the economy. So not only was the housing market booming, but the whole economy was stimulated. When the bubble burst, the amount of money decreased rapidly.

Some of the money simply evaporated. If a loan is defaulted on and the bank can't recover its money from selling the house, because house prices have fallen, then the bank has to write off its "asset" (the money you owed it). Money, loans and debts are only built on promises, it turns out. We'll look into that later. If I can't fulfil my promise, then it becomes worthless. If I gave you a piece of paper saying I owe you a pig, but my pig dies, then my promise, my piece of paper, is worthless to you. It's not necessarily anyone's fault, perhaps it's just from the vagaries of an unpredictable world. Promises involve risk, another theme we will pick up later.

Another reason the amount of money decreased is that more money was diverted into repaying loans. The sudden drop in money supply slowed business, reduced many incomes, and people had to stretch more to make their loan repayments. The sudden change to bad times made people more cautious, so they repaid loans faster than they might have otherwise, and they avoided taking out new loans. All of this further reduced the money supply. Business slowed further. Times became really bad.

This is why a Wall Street crash causes so much disruption on Main Street. It's because the money supply goes up and down as the financial markets go up and down. It's because new bank "loans" are made with new money created out of nothing. Other financial market dealings also effectively create new purchasing power. If the deals go bad, people on Main Street don't have as much money to spend.

By the way, this is not how it's supposed to work in the mythical version of capitalism. In the capitalist myth, the capitalist accumulates a lot of money (capital) and re-invests it. In the real modern world the capitalist borrows most of the money. So perhaps we should re-name the present regime *debtism* instead of capitalism.

It doesn't have to be this way. It is possible to create and issue money separately from making "loans", and then an investment failure wouldn't reduce the amount of money available. Then a Wall Street crash would mainly affect the investors and gamblers on Wall Street, and Main Street could carry on its routine business without much effect.

You won't hear this said very often. Changing the way money is supplied seems to be a deeply disreputable topic among economists. They avert their eyes and quickly change the subject. (Later they mutter "She's a bright lass, but dear oh dear, she'll never make it to Harvard.") I'm not sure why the topic is so odious, it seems like something that deserves to be debated. Of course the present system has allowed bankers and financiers to become masters of the universe, so that might have something to do with it.

Anyway, it seems I just explained the GFC in a couple of pages of fairly plain English. Certainly there were other factors involved, some more of which I'll mention shortly, but I think we've covered the essence. Yet it seems this explanation has never occurred to the economists in charge of major economies. There are reasons for that which I'll get to.

Some real-world evidence

Before going into that however I want to show it's not just theory. Steve Keen, the author of *Debunking Economics* mentioned earlier, is one of those fringe economists who actually has useful things to say, a lot of useful things. Figure 2.1 below is a graph he produced, showing the amount of available money that was supplied by new loans, as a percentage of Gross Domestic Product (the total amount spent in a year) in Australia and the US. Don't panic! I'll explain in words what it means. It's mostly harmless (the graph, not the meaning).

In 2007, around 20% of the money Australians spent was from net new borrowings. In other words, the net amount of borrowed money, loans obtained *minus* repayments on

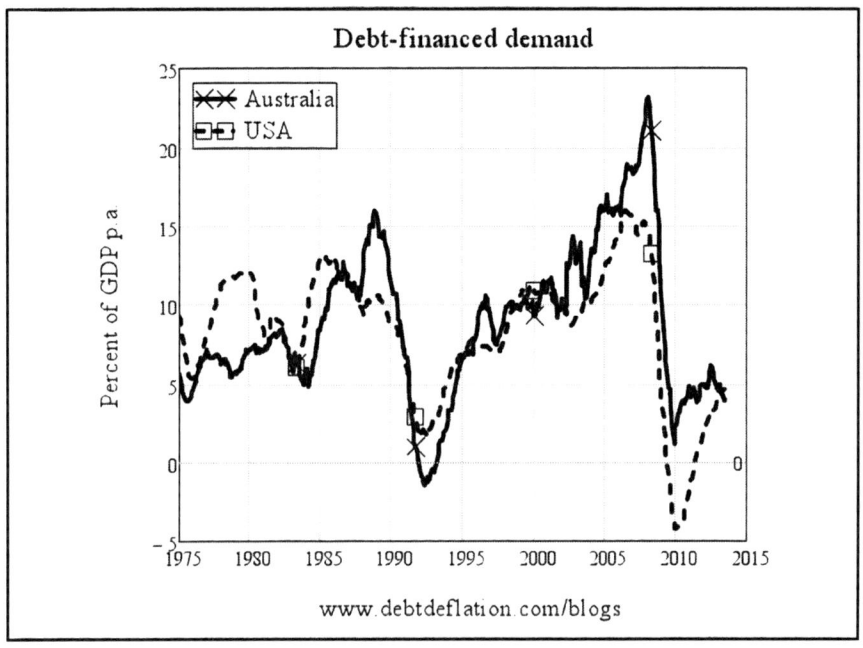

Figure 2.1. *The amount of available money (demand) due to increasing debt, as a percentage of GDP, for Australia and the US. From Keen[12].*

existing loans, amounted to about 20% of the total money we spent that year. You can see the curve for Australia peaks above 20% in 2007-8.

When I first realised we had borrowed so much of what we spent in 2007 (from an earlier graph of Keen's) my jaw dropped. Without that borrowing, the economy would have been in deep recession. Instead of the economy growing by a moderate 3-4% that year, it would have shrunk by 15% or more. It meant we were living off our credit cards. More precisely, we were living off our mortgage loans, because they were much the biggest component of the net new debt. So much for a healthy, booming economy. So much for having another world's greatest treasurer. So much for the Liberal-National Coalition government being great economic managers.

The situation in the US was nearly as bad. Their net new borrowing was around 10% per year for much of a decade, due first to the dot-com bubble in the late 1990s and then to the sub-prime mortgage bubble, during which it rose to 15%.

The bubbles burst in 2007-8. "Demand" (economese for how much money we have available to spend) plummeted by nearly 20% of GDP in the US, which quickly went into deep recession. Some people went broke and had little to spend, others stopped borrowing and started paying down their debts, banks stopped lending because of the high risk in a depressed economy and because people didn't want to borrow, and so on.

We survived better in Australia because the economists in the Reserve Bank, and Prime Minister Kevin Rudd, had a fit of sanity, to their great credit. They decided we'd be better off in the medium term if the government spent a lot of money, money that partially replaced what people had been borrowing. So they upgraded schools, helped people to insulate their homes and gave old people a one-off handout to tide them through the hard times. Most of this was sensible spending anyway, because schools and insulation are good investments that will pay back over time. As a result, our net private borrowing dropped to near zero (which should be normal and healthy) rather than going very negative as it did in the US.

This time Australia *did* have competent economic managers, though you'd never know it from the howling raised by the Opposition and most of the media ever since about "unsustainable" government debt. In the US, by contrast, the Federal Reserve, instead of spending money directly, dumped trillions of dollars into the vaults of the big banks. However the banks didn't loan it out for people to spend, because they didn't trust each other and because people didn't want to take on more debt. So the US dropped into deep recession and has not emerged yet.

Since the GFC, all the talk has been about the need to cut *government* debt, to get the government budget back in balance, because only then, supposedly, will economies recover. That is the approach in the Eurozone, in Britain and the US, and it is the approach the Opposition and the media would inflict on us in Australia. The funny thing is that *private* debt was much larger than government debt in most countries and still is. Private debt peaked in Australia at around 160% of GDP and in the US near 150% of GDP[3,12].

The government debts that all the chatter is about are much less. Government debt in the developed countries averages about 90% of GDP. In the US public debt was around 40% of GDP before the GFC, and has since risen to around 70%[13], far less than the private debt. Australian government debt is not commonly documented. One estimate puts it at about 11% of GDP[14], another at 20% of GDP[15]. These are very low numbers by any comparison, so it is ludicrous that there is a hysterical scare campaign, and that the present Government does not squash the fuss with a clear statement of the situation.

It was unsustainable *private* debt that caused the GFC. Australia was saved from recession because the government had the guts to go into debt so enough money would be circulating to keep Main Street business, also known as the productive economy, functioning. Europe and the US are still deep in recession because of *austerity* policies. Government debts must be repaid before the economy can revive, they claim. The results show clearly otherwise, as does the sensible interpretation of Keen. This is why Dean Baker was raging against "deficit hawks" in the quote in Chapter 1.

What counts most is not whether debt is public or private. What counts is whether borrowing is invested in sensible projects that will pay back over a reasonable time. School buildings and housing insulation are sensible investments. Dumping money into a property bubble is not a sensible investment.

Pyramids and Ponzi schemes

The huge increases of private debt were the result of property bubbles. The property bubbles occurred because of malfunctioning banks and because economists treat land as though it is just another producible commodity. (The difference between land and commodities is another worthy topic that will be taken up later.) Bank profits rise as people take out bank loans. In a short-sighted effort to boost profits, the banks became too generous in making loans. This allowed people to bid up the price of land. (People usually say the cost of housing, but it is the land component of the house-and-land package that inflates too readily.) The banks used the false equity of higher land prices to give even bigger loans. So land prices spiralled to ever higher values.

The process is like a pyramid scheme. Everyone is encouraged to "invest" in land. The price goes up, and those who buy and sell early make a windfall profit. Eventually there are no more suckers buying land, the price falls, and those who bought at inflated prices lose a lot of money. The net result is a transfer of money from some people to other people, but nothing productive has been accomplished. Worse, because the money supply is tied to debt levels, the economy as a whole booms, then busts, and misery is spread far and wide.

There are laws against pyramid schemes. The crudest pyramid scheme is when you are invited to send $100 to Joe Blow, in return for his priceless financial advice, and then invite ten other people to send $100 dollars to you. You can recoup your $100 and make $900 more by following the instructions, and so can they, so long as ten suckers can be found. Fairly soon there aren't enough suckers to keep it going, and a lot of people lose a lot of money.

A variation on the pyramid is the Ponzi scheme, named for the man who made grand promises to investors, then made big payments to early investors with funds received from later investors, without actually investing in anything useful. A recent practitioner of the Ponzi scheme was Bernie Madoff, who came unstuck (as they all do) during the GFC. He is the biggest fish so far prosecuted for illegal behaviour, defrauding investors of about $65 billion, but this is chicken feed compared to the losses from misbehaviour of the big finance and ratings firms.

Banks need to be restructured and regulated so they provide loans as a service, because at present they operate under a perverse incentive. The provision of loans is supposed to be a service, but the incentive is to push loans on people well beyond prudent levels of debt. There used to be something called "sound banking practice" (well, there is a myth by that name), and we need to ensure banks' incentives promote good behaviour. The financial sector really does not need to comprise more than a few percent of the economy. We'll see the arguments for that later. Instead, it dominates the real, productive economy, to everyone else's detriment.

By the way, I've been using the term *speculative bubble,* and talking about inflating the bubble, but it's a curious thing that this kind of inflation is not counted when economists calculate *the inflation rate*, the rate at which prices rise. If the price of oranges goes up, this counts as contributing to inflation. If the price of housing goes up, it isn't counted towards inflation. I've had occasion to ask an economist if this is really true, and why. The response has gone something like "Oh yes well ... technical reasons ... international comparisons ... mumble mumble ... OECD ... blah blah". But, I say, isn't it a major omission? After all, the rent or the mortgage payment is one of the biggest, often *the* biggest, expense for your average family. Buying the family home is the biggest investment most people make. More mumbling.

So in Australia, with the world's best-managed economy (perhaps), official inflation has been held between 2% and 4% for a couple of decades, yet the price of housing has doubled or tripled in that time. Actually it may be worse. I bought a house in 1983 for $54,000. Thirty years later the same house would cost around ten times as much. That's an average inflation rate of about 8%. There's another major market failure operating here, which we'll explore later, yet the effect of it is not even counted as inflation.

Of course politicians would panic if they thought someone was going to tell ordinary people they'd been experiencing much higher inflation than the official statistics show. Those official statistics would be the ones that prove we have the best-managed economy in the world. However ordinary people might not be so surprised, they know what they've been paying. Politicians and economists who lecture the electorate for being ungrateful and surly might do well to ponder whether the electorate knows better than they do.

I mentioned earlier there were more practices that drove the US bubble to absurd levels. They were all basically forms of speculation, but the big banks got terribly clever about it. Well, some practices were not clever at all. Banks gave loans to people increasingly unlikely to be able to repay them, even to unemployed people. They justified this to themselves by assuming they could always repossess a house and sell it for a higher price, thus recouping their investment. They were just playing a pyramid scheme. Banks are supposed to be smarter than that, but most of them apparently persuaded themselves they had to be in the game or they would be out-competed by other banks.

Even worse, these "sub-prime" loans, the ones to people who hardly had a pulse, were repackaged into complex bundles, with less risky loans and other bets on the market, in ways that were supposed not just to dilute the risk but to remove it. This was done by mathematicians and physicists who were so clever they were stupid. Compounding the stupidity, big ratings companies rated these "financial products" AAA, and big financial companies bought them. No-one could actually tell what was in the bundles, as they were put together by complicated computer programs. In all the excitement, no-one noticed the smell of dead fish.

So everyone persuaded themselves that giving mortgage loans to junkies could be made in a way that was risk-free. Their terribly clever manipulations completely disconnected the loans process from market feedback. In theory, when the junkies failed to make their payments, the bank would make a loss, reduce its loan portfolio and the price of houses would steady or fall gently. In practice this did not happen until the bad loans were spread through much of the global financial system. There was another market failure, a monumental one this time.

(Small, slightly technical aside. One main reason the supposedly risk-free bundles were too clever by half is they were based on the way the market had behaved in the past.

However when everyone started using the new bundles, the market was no longer like it was in the past. The very clever formulas no longer applied. You can extrapolate the past into the future, but there's no guarantee the future will be like the past. In fact hardly anyone has ever been known to actually predict the future. Anything involving the future involves risk. The "risk-free" packages were not risk free. Oops.)

All this cleverness kept gravity at bay for quite a long time. By the time the gravity police finally arrived to enforce the law, the dead fish had been spread through most of the global financial system. When one part fell, the whole lot threatened to come down. All the big banks knew all the other big banks didn't know how much risk they were actually carrying, and whether they might really be bankrupt, so they refused to deal with each other. The financial system went into gridlock.

The story after that is fairly well known. Trillions of dollars were dumped into the banks. A lot of the money was from taxpayers. A lot more was created out of nothing. In Europe this "recapitalising" of the banks was reasonably regarded as the government, on behalf of the public, taking a stake in the bank, and the government therefore required to have a say in how the bank was run. In the US the same practice was known by the dirty word *socialism,* so rather than sully their ideological purity they just *gave* the money to the banks. Either way the banks said "thank you very much" and soon their executives and traders were back to making squillions in bonuses.

Many of the newly-impoverished middle class were not making squillions. Many of the already-impoverished poor moved onto the street. Later, when some people moved onto Wall Street, they were attacked by police. The police did not enquire much into the illegality occurring, on a monumental scale, within the big buildings along Wall Street.

Bankers' blindness

What were mainstream economists doing during all this bubbling and bursting? First, assuring us everything was fine, even as the unravelling began. Then, being astonished and bewildered.

Jean-Phillipe Cotis, chief economist of the OECD, said in May, 2007, after the sub-prime mortgage industry had already collapsed, early bank victims had already fallen and economies were slowing

> … the current situation is in many ways better than we have experienced in years. … Our central forecast remains indeed quite benign: a soft landing in the United States, a strong and sustained recovery in Europe … sustained growth in the OECD economies would be underpinned by strong job creation and falling unemployment.[3]

By November 2007, Lehman Brothers was no more and the financial system was in gridlock. Recently the official unemployment rate in the Eurozone reached 12.1%. In Spain unemployment is over 25%.

Former Chairman of the US Federal Reserve, Alan Greenspan, allowed in October 2008

> Those of us who have looked to the self-interest of lending institutions to protect shareholders' equity, myself included, are in a state of shocked disbelief. The whole intellectual edifice, however, collapsed in the summer of last year.

Shocked disbelief. Later, Greenspan recovered himself. By April 2011 he was arguing against proposals to modestly regulate the financial sector, claiming in effect that financial machinations were far too complex for regulators to understand, so they shouldn't try. He further managed to imply that the GFC and the Great Recession are an aberration.

In 1998 a hedge fund called, with wonderful irony, Long Term Capital Management, almost brought the global financial system down single-handed. Later Martin Gruber, Nomura Professor of Finance at New York University's Stern School and a friend of the Nobel-Prize-winning perpetrators, said:

> A series of events occurred that were outside the norm. These catastrophes happen. The fault isn't with the models.[16]

So if the fault isn't with the models, where does the fault lie? The only other possibility is with reality. Reality was at fault.

Outside the norm, an aberration: economists cannot be expected to explain or predict such things, don't be ridiculous. That quickly became the standard defence after the GFC. They claimed the GFC came from nowhere, that it was not a foreseeable event. Some went so far as to call it a Black Swan event[17], something so far outside our experience that you would not think to imagine it, just as Europeans would not have thought of swans being black before they explored Australia and found black swans. If that were true, there would not be much that could be done. How do you guard against the inconceivable?

The trouble is quite a few economists *did* see the GFC coming, and they were presenting plausible evidence for their predictions well before it happened. Of course there are always a few people predicting doom of one sort or another, and some of those predictions are likely to be about economic doom. So the chances are when something bad happens someone will claim to have predicted it. However they often don't say how often their predictions have been wrong, or whether it was just dumb luck they made their prediction at the right time. So it's important to look at the basis of the predictions and the record of the predictor.

Suffice to say here that a number of people offered rather straightforward, clear and readily-available evidence for their predictions, such as record levels of private debt or high fractions of incomes going into mortgages. That is why three of the predictors (Steve Keen, Noriel Roubini and Dean Baker) were given *Revere Awards* by a group that has since become the World Economics Association[18]. The award is named in honour of Paul Revere and his famous ride through the night to warn Americans of the approaching British army.

If some economists did see a crisis looming, using readily available information, then apparently most economists were not looking in the right place, or they would have seen the problem too. There's the old story of the drunk looking for his car keys under a street light. When a passer-by asks where he might have lost them the drunk points into the dark down the street. "Then why are you looking here, you should be looking down there." "Ah" replies the drunk, "but it's too dark down there, you'd never be able to see them."

Keen, Roubini and Baker used data that shed light out in the "dark" where the problem was developing (as I'll show shortly). Why, then, were most economists only looking in the wrong place, under the street light where there was no problem?

This brings us to one of the more fundamental flaws in mainstream economics (though there are several others equally fundamental). The answer is that most economists consider private debt has no effect on the economy. This might seem a little odd, given the discussion we've already been through.

Economists claim *one person's debt is another person's asset.* In plain language they mean the money you borrowed from the bank came from someone who saved their money in the bank. While you are spending their money, supposedly, they can't spend it. So the net effect on the total economy is zero. The only effect is that you are spending the money rather than them. Conversely, when you are repaying you have to do without, but they can resume spending.

However this is not how bank loans work, as we have seen. When a bank gives you a loan, only a small fraction of the money comes from someone else's savings. Ninety percent or more of the loan is new money created out of nothing. Your loan increases the total purchasing power in the economy. You have new money to spend, and no-one is having to do without their hard-earned savings. This is why the economy goes up and down as the financial markets go up and down.

Perhaps the claim *one person's debt is another person's asset* might apply more to the stock market? If it were only savings that were invested in stocks, that would be true. However a lot of bank loans are used in new business ventures. It also seems that many of the clever derivative "instruments" created in the financial markets can be exchanged in payments, and so are effectively money, of a limited kind, which also increases purchasing power. Without delving into the labyrinths of high finance, it is clear the state of the financial markets affects the state of the economy. So the level of private debt is important.

Of the economists who did warn of the approaching crisis, Steve Keen's case was one of the clearest and best documented[3]. He was alerted to the problem in 2005 when he plotted official data on private debt and GDP in Australia over a long period. Figure 2.2 shows the ratio of private debt to GDP.

From about 1964 the ratio began a long, roughly exponential increase. In 2005 it was already above 125%, well

Figure 2.2. The ratio of private debt to GDP in Australia from 1860 to 2011[3,12].

above the level reached in the Great Depression, and above the even higher peak reached in the 1890s depression. The ratio peaked around 160%, and it has hovered around 150% since. This is still a high level of debt to be carrying, though at least it has ceased its precipitous rise. (Technical notes: It was from this graph, that I saw private debt had increased by 20% of GDP in 2007 and realised we were living off borrowings. At about the same time Keen began using the rate of increase of the curve as a measure of debt exposure, and that is what is plotted in Figure 2.1.)

So mainstream economists overlooked the approaching private debt crisis because they have been taught private debt does not matter. As a result they weren't looking in the right place when trouble started to develop. The data were readily

31

available, but apparently they never thought to plot them the way Keen did, or they did not consider them significant. That is why the GFC took them by surprise.

There is something strange here. On the one hand, economists say one person's debt is another person's asset. On the other hand the economics texts explain the fractional reserve system, which involves the creation of new money in the loans process, which contradicts the first claim. I don't know why the contradiction is not noticed, but it is not the only fundamental inconsistency in mainstream economics.

The blindness to the role of private debt is not confined to interpreting graphs like Figure 2.2. *Debt and money are excluded* from the computer models used by economists to monitor and forecast the state of the economy. Debt is excluded for the false reason already stated: one person's debt is another person's asset, so the total purchasing power in the economy is not affected. Money is excluded because, it is claimed, money only facilitates exchange, so it is like a lubricant to the economy. Money removes some friction from the economy, but does not play any active role in driving the economy. It is a neutral intermediary, they claim.

But *money is a form of debt.* Your ten dollar note is an implicit social contract that carries an implicit promise. If you received it from your boss in return for work you did for him, he has the value of your work but you only have a piece of paper that you can't eat. The paper only has value because the grocery store will recognise the implicit promise it carries: "the community owes the bearer goods or services to the value of ten dollars". We will explore the nature of money later, along with alternative ways money might be supplied. The point here is that all debt carries risk, because all debt implies a promise about the future, and no-one can predict the future.

So money is not a neutral lubricant in the economy. Money is debt and carries risk, just as much as a bank loan or a clever instrument of the financial markets. Money can actively drive the economy, as we will explore later.

So the big, elaborate computer models that are used to monitor and predict the economy exclude absolutely fundamental aspects of the economy from their number crunching: debt and money. (They also have the built-in assumption that the economy is always close to equilibrium, something equally amazing, but we'll take that up later.) It was this kind of computer model that misled Jean-Phillipe Cotis of the OECD to proclaim, as the collapse was already under way, "Our central forecast remains indeed quite benign".

The invisible foot

This chapter has identified a number of shortcomings of mainstream economic thinking. These involve both theoretical concepts that are erroneous or that exclude fundamental factors, and observations that are clearly at odds with economic theories and models. Thus a speculative bubble is a signature of a market failure. Bank loans increase the money supply. Debts are contracts involving the future, and so intrinsically involve risk. Money is a form of debt. Modern "capitalism" is not driven by accumulations of capital, it is driven by huge levels of borrowing, so it should be called "debtism". Government debts are small compared with private debt, and much less important. Inflation of house (or land) prices is not counted in official inflation rates. The deregulated financial markets found many clever ways to block market signals for longer and longer, and thus magnify the market failure. The financial sector is much bigger than it needs to be.

Land is not a producible commodity. If the world does not follow the predictions of economic models, it is the world that is at fault. Economists know their prescriptions for deregulated markets are correct, so any problem must be temporary and an aberration, whatever that might mean.

Most economists are not *complete* fundamentalists about markets. To varying degrees they allow that there are such things as market "imperfections". I have not used that term because I think a nearly complete malfunction of the financial markets, that causes misery for hundreds of millions if not billions of people, is not appropriately described as an "imperfection", or an "aberration". Markets are powerful, but they can fail utterly, or they can function in ways that benefit only a few at the expense of everyone else.

Economists' favourite metaphor is of the *invisible hand.* Supposedly, the market acts as an invisible hand, guiding society to the best possible collective outcome even as everyone is busy simply pursuing their own self interest. Well a market crash is a result that hurts society as a whole. Some more enlightened economists have said such bad effects are the due to the action of the *invisible foot.* We will see later there is no reason to expect markets always to be the benign hand, they are just as likely to be the destructive foot.

By the way, economists commonly attribute the invisible hand metaphor to Adam Smith, but they vastly overstate the significance he attributed to it. He did at one point say that an entrepreneur, in choosing domestic over foreign investment, can sometimes be guided as if by an invisible hand: "… each person, by following only his own self interest, is led by an invisible hand to promote an end which was no part of his intention". However he certainly didn't imply that markets always have this benign effect. His remark was actually in the context of railing against mercantilists (read global corporations) and government making cosy monopolist deals to the detriment of English society, particularly when England was drawn into wars to extend or defend colonies[19]. Still a pertinent concern. Smith has been grossly misrepresented by the modern profession. Add ignorance of its own history to the deficiencies of mainstream economics.

The further exploration of these themes, and others equally astounding, is pursued in following chapters. Markets are clearly powerful, and there are ways of fixing many of the failures of the present misguided *laissez-faire* regime. There are also areas where markets are not appropriate, and there are obviously legitimate roles for government, which is just meant to be the expression of our collective will. These themes will also be explored in what follows.

3

ROCKING CHAIR
OR WILD HORSES?

NEOCLASSICAL economists, the ones who dominate mainstream economics, believe economies are almost always close to a *general equilibrium* in which all supplies balance all demands. They believe this because it is the central prediction of the *neoclassical theory* of free markets. This theory also predicts that the general equilibrium is the most efficient state the economy could possibly achieve. By efficient, economists mean you get the greatest production of goods and services from a given input of resources and effort.

If this were true of real markets, prices and wages would always be fair, there would be full employment and market crashes would be impossible. We would be getting rich at the fastest possible rate. The only things that would disturb this blessed state would be external shocks like natural disasters and wars, or new technologies.

Gentle rocking?

In October 1987 stock markets around the world dropped by 25-40% within a day. There was no war. There was no great earthquake or tsunami. Thirty percent of the world's factories had not been bombed overnight. We had not suddenly forgotten how to work our modern technologies. There was no identifiable external cause of the sudden drop in the perceived value of stocks.

The only change, the explanation for the drop in stock prices, was within the minds of stock market traders. One day they thought values were high. The next day they thought the values were low, so they sold stock and prices plummeted. The invisible foot did its work. It was a classic market crash, and it was due to internal forces within the stock market.

Sometimes a picture conveys something in a way that words do not, even 1000 words. It is one thing to say the market crashed within a single day, it is another to convey quite how anomalous that was. So, knowing we don't have to panic if another graph makes an appearance, here is a graph that conveys the message rather, well, graphically.

Figure 3.1(a) shows what the 1987 crash looked like, in terms of the US Dow-Jones Industrial Average of stock prices, 1986-89. The drop is clearly big, and very sudden, even compared with the short-term jumping around that the Dow does most of the time. You can also see there was a relatively rapid rise in the Dow over the previous year. (Figure 3.1 includes parts (b) and (c), which relate to various attempts to interpret the crash. We'll get them to soon.)

Mainstream economists also believe in something called the *efficient markets hypothesis*. This is the claim that financial market traders collectively bring all relevant information to bear, and therefore the market prices can be expected to accurately represent the "true" value of the entities being traded. This, it is claimed, will be true even though any individual trader knows only a fraction of the relevant information. In turn, efficient markets would ensure capital is allocated with maximum effectiveness to enterprises. It would further imply that stock markets will be close to the optimal equilibrium state, in the absence of external disturbances.

The trouble is, markets will be efficient in this sense only if traders act totally independently from each other. Unfortunately, in real life, it is well known that traders follow trends at least as much as they try to base their trades on "fundamentals", that is on the actual state of the entity being traded. In other words, they commonly follow the herd, rather than acting independently. In that case there is no basis for claiming markets allocate capital efficiently.

How do you reconcile the 1987 rise and fall of stock prices with the idea that the stock market is always close to equilibrium? You can't. You would have a hard time arguing prices were in equilibrium the day before the crash. The most you might try to claim is the market returned to equilibrium during the crash, but that implies it was far from equilibrium before the crash. However there's not really any clear way to know what the equilibrium price might have been.

Some possibilities are illustrated in Figure 3.1(b), where some possible "equilibrium" trend lines have been added. They slope upward to the right, allowing for an underlying trend to rising values. But which is the correct underlying trend? And where, vertically, might the equilibrium trend be? There's no way of knowing. The only thing you can conclude from the graph is the market was a long way from equilibrium before the crash, or after the crash, or both. For an average crash around the world by about 30%,

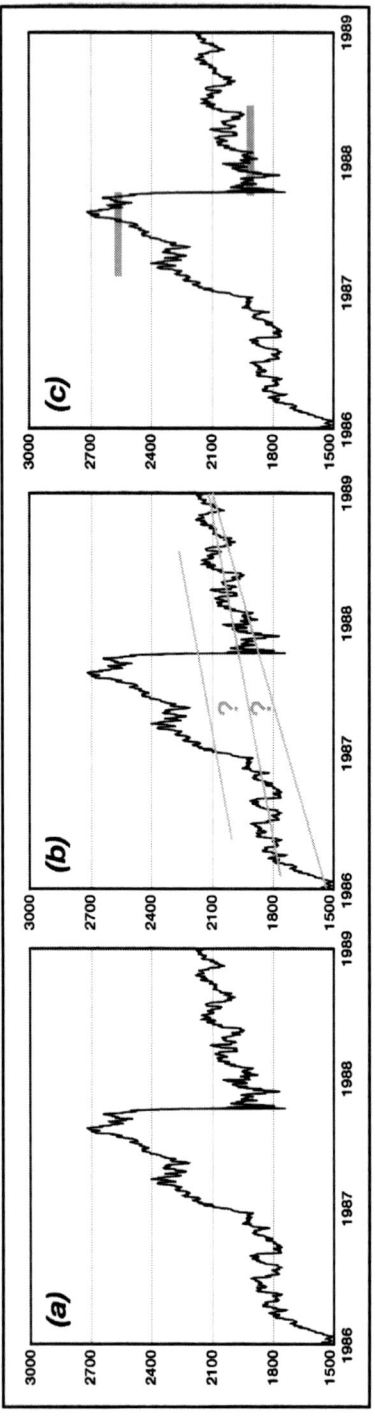

Figure 3.1 (a) US Dow-Jones Industrial Average of stock prices, 1986-89. From Colombo[20]. (b) Putative equilibrium trend lines. (c) Before-and-after equilibria, of the kind assumed by Eggertsson and Krugman[21] for the GFC.

this means the stock market was at least 15% away from equilibrium, and possibly 30%. Those are big imbalances.

Figure 3.1(c) illustrates, conceptually, an approach taken by Gauti B. Eggertsson (of the New York Federal Reserve) and

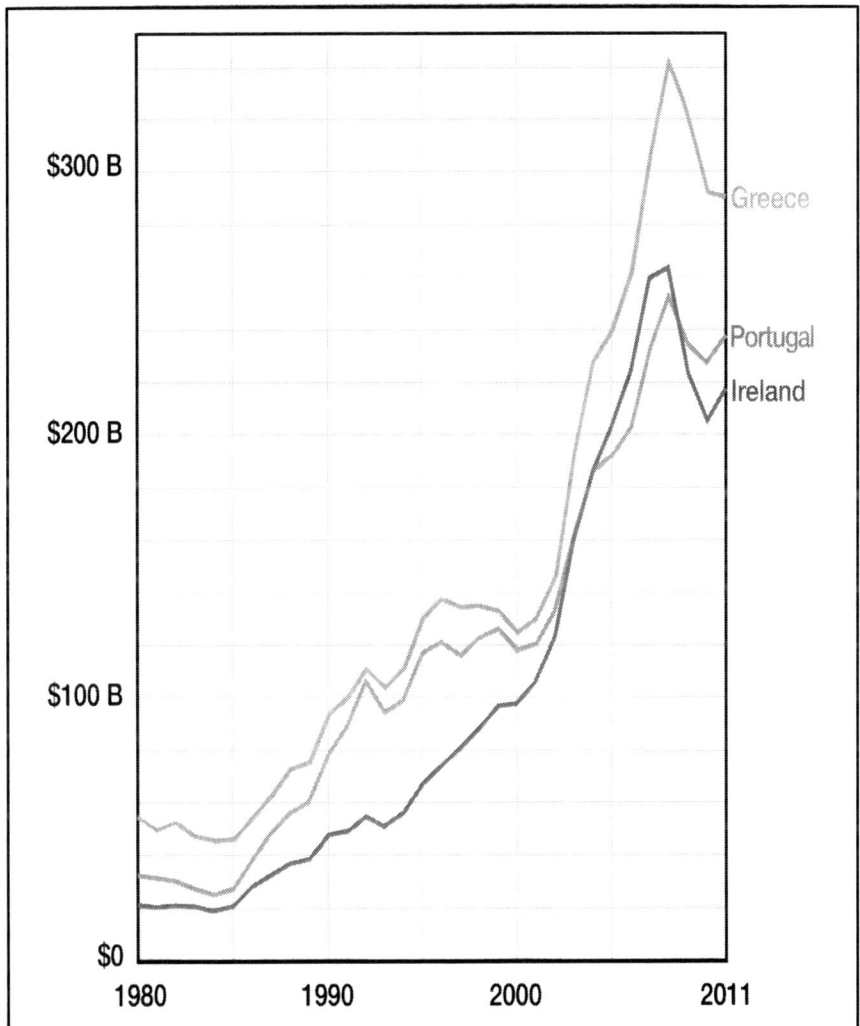

Figure 3.2. *GDP of several Euro-area countries, 1980-2011: Greece, Portugal, Ireland. The details are not important, just the overall pattern of rise, followed by the fall after 2008 due to the Global Financial Crisis. Data from the World Bank.*

Paul Krugman (Nobel Laureate, New York Times columnist, and professor at Princeton University), who attempted to apply neoclassical equilibrium modelling to the Global Financial Crisis[21]. In what is apparently regarded as a very innovative paper, they allowed that there must have been some disequilibrium during the GFC crash. Their neoclassical methods could not directly address the decline during the crash, because the markets were then out of equilibrium. So they made equilibrium models for before the crash and after the crash and tried to say something about the change that had occurred between the *before* and *after* states. The graphical illustration of this approach in Figure 3.1(c) ought to make it obvious there's no good reason to assume the markets were in equilibrium at either time, but especially before the crash. Another example we'll get to soon will make this point quite explicitly.

The Global Financial Crisis was similar in general character to the 1987 crash, as is evident in Figure 3.2, which shows the GDPs of several European countries in the lead up to and through the crisis. The fall is not as large or abrupt as in 1987, but still the pattern is a relatively rapid rise followed by a fall back.

Overshoot and crash

A pattern like this is very familiar in other fields of knowledge. Ecologists know it as the overshoot-and-crash phenomenon. Sometimes animals like locusts or rabbits breed rapidly until they exceed the carrying capacity of the land. However they sometimes keep breeding and eating until there is no food left at all. At that point many of them starve, and the population suddenly drops. Unfortunately the ecosystem will have been severely damaged by their ravages, so the amount of food is much less than it was before the population boom. Although some of the animals survive, there will be many fewer of them unless and until the carrying capacity of the land can recover. Had the population stopped rising as it approached the carrying capacity, many more animals could have lived on the land.

A debt-fuelled boom and bust can be described in much the same terms. People take on more and more debt, until they exceed the reasonable capacity of the economy to carry the cost and risk of the borrowing. However, driven on by speculation or a wish not to be left behind, they keep borrowing, until the level of debt exceeds the capacity of many people to repay at all. At that point there is a cascade of defaults and the amount of debt rapidly decreases. Unfortunately, because the supply of money to Main Street is tied to the debt markets, the contraction of the money supply damages the productive economy. So even though the amount of debt decreases, the ability of the economy to carry debt also decreases, and people end up worse off than before the bubble started. It may then take a long time for the productive economy to recover its carrying capacity.

Ecologists have been doing calculations of population booms and busts for a long time, and the approach can be readily adapted to a debt-driven boom and bust. An example is shown in Figure 3.3. Interestingly, with a small adjustment of parameters we can also obtain the case where the debt levels off smoothly at the economy's carrying capacity. We can even get a case where there is only a small overshoot, followed by oscillations above and below the carrying capacity. All three cases are included in Figure 3.3.

There is quite a lot to learn from this graph, so before the panic sets in let's take some deep breaths and walk slowly through the key features. The thick lines are for the case where the level of debt smoothly approaches the carrying capacity of the economy. The amount of debt is shown as the thick, solid line, and the carrying capacity as the thick dashed line, which is just horizontal at the value 1. The calculation is done assuming the net rate of issuing of loans starts out increasing by a fixed percentage per year, in this case 15%. However as the amount of debt approaches the carrying capacity, the net rate of issuing loans decreases, becoming zero at the carrying capacity. This causes the amount of debt to smoothly level off at the carrying capacity.

The resulting steady state, where the level of debt equals the carrying capacity, is an equilibrium state. The supply of debt just balances the demand for debt. A neoclassical near-equilibrium model might cope with this state. However it could not cope with the initial build up of debt, which is well out of balance.

In the case just considered, everyone is well-behaved. The bankers only offer loans to people who can comfortably repay them, and people only take on loans within their comfortable capacity. As the overall level of debt approaches the carrying capacity, everyone becomes more cautious, until new loans are only taken out at the rate old loans are paid off.

But what happens if people are not so prudent. What if the banks keep pushing loans to increase their profits, and speculators buy low and just want the price to keep rising so they can sell high? What if legitimate home buyers also take on loans that are above their comfort level so they don't get left behind? Then the feedback from the market would be ignored. As the amount of debt rises above the comfortable carrying capacity, people start to default, but no-one pays much attention. What if they don't pay attention until two more years have elapsed, and defaults are becoming frequent?

The second case in Figure 3.3, shown in the medium-thickness lines, shows what happens if the feedback that slows the rate of issuing new loans is delayed by two years. Then the level of debt overshoots, and only peaks two years later. It then falls because, in this story, defaults occur in proportion to the amount of overshoot, and are also delayed. So defaults continue as the level of debt falls through the carrying capacity, and there is an undershoot. Then the process repeats, but with smaller overshoot and undershoot. In this example, neither the overshoot nor the undershoot are very large, and the level of debt oscillates about the ideal level.

This is an interesting case because it resembles what is called "the business cycle", in which the economy periodically "overheats", inflation starts to rise, interest rates are increased to slow things down and, not unusually, there is an overcorrection and the economy may slip into a mild recession. The process can then repeat. Though there are more things involved than just the level of debt, such as the level of inventories and of investment in new plant and dwellings, the effect of these other factors is of the same general kind.

Now let's get to the third case in Figure 3.3. In this case (shown by the thin lines), the delay in market feedback taking effect is extended to 3.5 years. The result is not just oscillations somewhat larger than in the previous case (by a factor 3.5/2 = 1.75). Rather, the result is an overshoot more than three times larger and a subsequent undershoot back to very low levels of debt. It takes about 15 years for the debt to regrow from such a low level.

During that time the economy would have less capital available, so it would be under-performing. Businesses, and people's lives, would also have been disrupted, and they might take time to generate new work and begin to perform again at their full capacity. I have represented this as a reduction in the economy's capacity to carry debt. I assumed the capacity declines in proportion to the amount of overshoot, and then recovers slowly, at 1% per year. In this third case the capacity drops to only about 85% of its initial value (thin dashed line). It then takes about 15 years to recover. In the second case (above) the economy is not damaged much by the slow down, and the capacity falls by less than 5% and recovers within a few years.

This third case resembles a major recession or a depression. To be sure it is a very simplified calculation, but it has crucial features in common with a real economy. Most importantly, it is clear the level of debt is a long way from the equilibrium value most of the time. In fact it is furthest from equilibrium at the peak and the trough. These are just the points at which Eggertsson and Krugman tried to apply equilibrium models, so their models cannot capture what is really going on. At the peak, the economy has become more and more precarious, and the higher the debt rises the larger the fall will be. Equilibrium models can tell you nothing about such large imbalances.

A very interesting feature of the calculations (or the mathematical "model", as we can also call it) is that it can explain a range of possible states: a steady economy, an economy with a kind of business cycle, or a depression, with just a change of one parameter. Mainstream economics has struggled for decades even to get a plausible business cycle, let alone a depression, out of its models. In fact it really can't, because even a business cycle involves substantial departures from equilibrium.

The model used for Figure 3.3 is very simple, and some of the assumptions are only educated guesses. Yet it has the potential to be built upon such that it could become a very useful model. More variables could be included, and the relationships among them could be based more explicitly on observed relationships. One can have confidence that if the relationships imply disequilibrium, overshoot and crash, then the equations of the model will be capable of demonstrating such behaviour. Keen has in fact been pursuing such models, with some success[22].

On the other hand the neoclassical equilibrium models are not capable of following the far-from-equilibrium dynamical behaviour of an economy, no matter how complicated or sophisticated they are made. One of the currently popular kinds of models is called DSGE – Dynamic Stochastic General Equilibrium. Don't be fooled by the "Dynamic", it is still an equilibrium model, just one

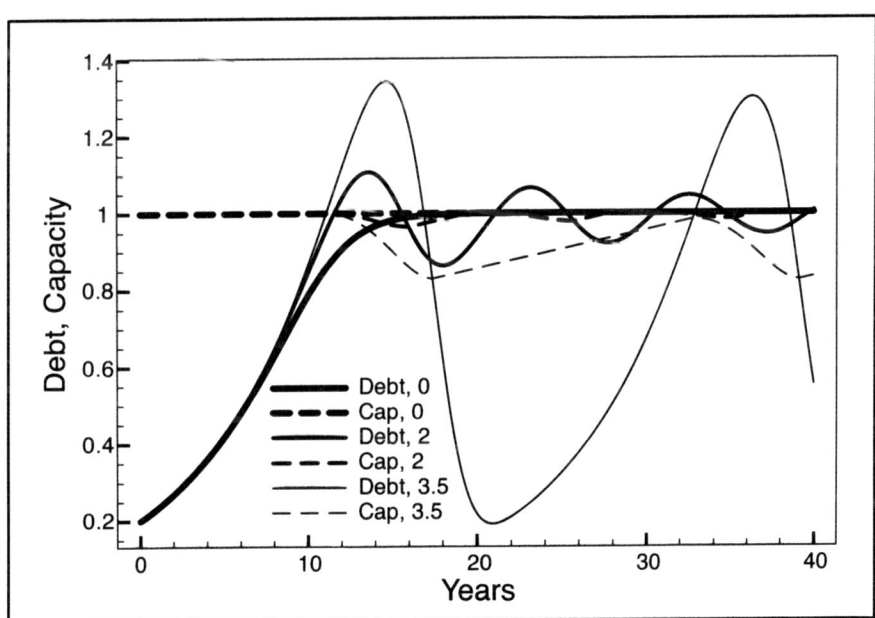

Figure 3.3. Amount of debt, relative to the "carrying capacity" of the economy, for three different cases: a smooth approach to the carrying capacity, a small overshoot followed by oscillations about the carrying capacity, and a large overshoot followed by a big drop, from which it takes a long time to recover. "Cap" is the capacity for each case. The number in the legend is the delay, in years, in the feedback signal. Details are explained in the main text.

that can change slowly. Physicists would recognise this approach as quasi-static. Not static, changing, but changing only slowly, so the relationships that apply at equilibrium still hold, to a good approximation. The models still can't properly describe a boom and bust cycle.

If you have a tray with tall glasses of beer on it, you can carry the tray without spilling the beer, so long as you're careful not to accelerate the tray too much. That would be quasi-static behaviour. However if you're on a train and the driver suddenly hits the brakes, you and the tray will depart a long way from equilibrium, the glasses will fall, and your friends will not be pleased. The GFC was a big jolt that spilt everyone's beer. Neoclassical economists had been practicing being good waiters on firm ground, but they were quite unprepared for the train to jerk under them.

In fact there are plenty of reasons to conclude that modern economies are *always* far from equilibrium. New technologies and new firms are bubbling up all the time. Vast amounts of money are zapped around the world at a frenetic rate. National economies are buffeted this way and that. We'll explore more of these features more as we go.

To readers familiar with some other fields of knowledge, such as population dynamics, engineering control systems, physical systems of many kinds from ice sheet collapses to the formation of star clusters and galactic arms, and many other examples, this discussion will appear unsurprising and perhaps a little trivial. *Of course* you can model an overshoot and crash phenomenon, of course it is far from equilibrium, and of course it involves nonlinear relationships as well. This sort of thing has been known and understood, in general terms, for a long time. If mainstream economists had not been so insular for so long, they would know about such things.

Mainstream economists are also likely to regard Figure 3.3 as trivial, and perhaps to dismiss it out of hand, but for a different reason. A calculation so simple could not *possibly* capture anything important about something as complex as an economy. To do that you need the elaborate and sophisticated mathematics of the neoclassical tradition. However if the neoclassical calculations leave out crucial features of real economies, like disequilibrium and key nonlinear relationships, then they can *never* reproduce the features shown in Figure 3.3, no matter how sophisticated and elaborate they are made.

This comparison reveals another fundamental deficiency of mainstream economics. It has never understood that, for a scientist, mathematics is only a tool. To do science, the essence is to deduce the implications of your hypotheses, and then to see if they have a *useful resemblance* to the observable world. It is this *testing against observations* of the world that is the essence of science. Mathematics is very useful for deducing the implications of a hypothesis, but how much mathematics is needed depends very much on the context. Sometimes a very simple estimate can be very instructive. Sometimes sophisticated mathematics or elaborate computations are justified, if enough of the complications of the system are reasonably understood, or if relevant observations have high precision.

Neoclassical economists seem to have missed that essence of science at the beginning, over a century ago. They have spent a century thinking that because they had an elegant theory about which you can do a lot of sophisticated mathematics, then they were doing science. No, they have been doing a lot of mathematics, but it does not have a useful resemblance to the observable world, so it is not science. It is, in simple terms, pseudo-science.

Origins of equilibrium theory

The neoclassical theory of free markets originated late in the nineteenth century[23]. For its time, it was a bold theory, an attempt to come up with a theory of societies as profound and rigorous as Newton's theory of gravity. Perhaps it could have been recognised even then that the behaviour of people is likely to be more complex than the behaviour of planets and falling apples. Nevertheless it was probably worth having a go, to see how well such a theory might do. It was actually modelled after some physics, the theory of how bouncing atoms give rise to the behaviour of gases, which come to an equilibrium of uniform pressure for a given volume and temperature. Put simplified people in place of atoms, consider only simplified interactions among people, go through the manipulations, and you get a system that comes to an equilibrium that optimises productivity.

The subsequent history of the two theories, of atoms and people, is instructive. Physicists quickly established that the bouncing-atoms theory of a "perfect gas" is pretty accurate for gases well above their condensation (and boiling) temperature. The closer the temperature is to condensation, the less accurate the theory becomes. Below the condensation temperature the gas transforms to a liquid, whose properties are very different from those of the gas, and the theory is so inaccurate as to be useless. Colder still and the liquid freezes into a solid, with another big change in properties. Some decades later, after the invention of quantum mechanics, it was found many properties of solids could be explained by taking account of quantum interactions among atoms, which are much more complex than those of the little bouncing spheres that were assumed for the perfect gas theory.

50

Economists, on the other hand, had a severe case of physics envy. They were so taken with the invention of a quantitative theory of people's interactions they became engrossed in exploring its properties and adding refinements. They did recognise that the prediction of an optimal equilibrium depended on some questionable assumptions. They therefore devoted enormous efforts, over many decades, to finding ways in which the general equilibrium could be preserved, even with less questionable assumptions. However they seem to have lost sight of an even more important question: is there any evidence the economy is close to equilibrium, at least some of the time? In light of a succession of financial malfunctions over the previous few centuries and into the twentieth century, one might have thought this was a fairly obvious question to address.

So you can see the problem. They liked the result of the early neoclassical theory so much they became infatuated with it. The question whether it bears any useful resemblance to real economies was neglected. Not entirely neglected, because there is a large field called econometrics that purports, in part, to compare theory and real world. However the effort seems commonly directed to finding ways in which the real world seems to resemble the theory, rather than to identifying ways in which the theory clearly does not resemble the real world. Never mind a lot of fancy statistics on market fluctuations during "normal" times, the 1987 crash is very obviously incompatible with the central prediction of the theory. The theory therefore has to be fundamentally questioned.

It is not hard to identify why the neoclassical theory does not usefully resemble real economies. It is because of the assumptions it is built on. Any theory, in physics, economics, or any field, is built on a set of assumptions about how the world works. You choose the assumptions as a compromise between how you think the world might work and how hard the mathematics, or computations, will be when you try to deduce the implications of your assumptions. The art of a good theory, and there is some art, is to find one that is mathematically tractable and whose assumptions give usefully accurate results.

Here are some of the assumptions upon which mainstream free market theory is built. We are all fully informed about every product and service we buy (so we will never buy a lemon, never be defrauded, never make an unwise investment). We are all rational, so we are not influenced by fashion, our peers or advertising (and of course the advertising industry simply chooses to waste all of its billions of dollars in its vain attempt to shift our preferences). We all have the same preferences – rich, poor, accountants, hippies, farmers, men ... err, women? We can all foretell the future. Well, that's not really true. No, it is assumed only that we can all assign accurate probabilities to all the possible future courses of events, though we don't actually need to know which events will transpire (so market players will always anticipate a possible crash, adjust their transactions and thereby ensure a crash never happens). There are no economies of scale (so apparently Henry Ford and Bill Gates got rich by sheer genius and not by gaining an early advantage, through cleverness or luck, and then undercutting smaller competitors by taking advantage of economies of scale).

That was a pretty quick run through some assumptions and some of their immediate implications. It should convey the idea that there are not just a couple of questionable assumptions, but many. However it's worth looking at some of them in a little more detail, not only to see if they might be usefully realistic in any way, but also because we can get some clues as to what we might predict if we make different assumptions.

Runaway growth

A good place to start is with economies of scale, because it's easy to see what would happen if you change the assumption. The neoclassical theory is built on an assumption that there are no economies of scale beyond a *point of diminishing returns.* An economy of scale means the more widgets you make, the less is the cost of production per widget.

Henry Ford did not invent assembly lines, but he was one of the first to take great advantage of their efficiencies. If you only wanted to build one Model-T Ford, you would not set up an assembly line, because assembly lines cost a lot to set up. However once you have set up an assembly line, including training workers to do all the various specialised jobs along the line, then you can make a Model-T for much less cost than before. Of course you have to cover the large initial cost of the assembly line, so you want to sell a lot of cars, so the initial cost can be recovered from many sales instead of one. If you sell enough cars, the average cost per car will fall below the cost of making one without an assembly line. If you sell more cars than that "break-even" point, you will be able to undercut your rivals by selling your cars for less than they sell theirs.

Once you have passed the break-even point, economists say you are gaining an economy of scale: as the *scale* of your operation gets bigger, so it becomes more *economical* to make more cars. (Technical aside: economists actually talk about *increasing returns to scale,* allowing that not only costs but prices may change systematically with scale. What counts is the difference between price and cost, in other words profit or *return* on investment.)

Let's get to the point. Once Henry Ford had his assembly line going, and had sold enough cars to pass the break-even point, then he could undercut his rivals. But with lower prices, he would sell more cars. But that would allow him to spread the initial cost even more thinly, over more cars, and lower his prices even further. Then he would sell even more cars ... . At one point Ford cars accounted for about half of the US car market. Ford's operation grew at the expense of many smaller ones, until he dominated the market.

According to the neoclassical theory, Ford should not have been able to dominate the market. You see the neoclassical theory is built on the assumption that economies of scale, if they exist at all, only exist up to a *point of diminishing returns*. Beyond that point, the bigger the scale of your operation the higher the average unit costs would be, in other words the higher the average cost per car. If that were true, then Ford's operation would have grown to a certain size and would then have stopped growing, because his costs would have been greater for each car he produced, and he would no longer be able to undercut his rivals.

There is an additional assumption, not so often stated explicitly, that the point of diminishing returns occurs before a company has become large enough to dominate its market. If this were also true, then perhaps Ford could have captured, say, ten percent of the market. Then other companies, seeing Ford's success, could imitate him and they might grow to about that size also. Then you would have ten or more manufacturers competing for your custom. *Then* (perhaps) healthy competition would ensue, the invisible hand would do its work, and the people would be blessed with the most and cheapest cars for the least input of materials and labour.

The problem for the neoclassical theory is that the invisible hand only works if no-one dominates the market. In a monopoly, the monopolist can charge whatever the market will bear, which may be far above his production costs, and he can become obscenely rich (and powerful, and buy himself compliant legislators, until you have a fascist fusion of big business and government). *Worse,* though, much worse, the market will not be *efficient.* Oh, the shame.

Well before you have monopoly conditions, you begin to have market failure. Even with ten manufacturers, it would not be hard to form an industry lobby group to press for a tariff on imports of your product. This, of course, would be to save the jobs of your workers (for whose welfare you care deeply, and who vote for your legislator) from unscrupulous foreign dealers. (Incidentally, an industry lobby group is another illustration that competition and cooperation are not mutually exclusive.)

Henry Ford's assembly line is famous precisely because it demonstrated the power of economies of scale. Microsoft famously spent tens of millions of dollars promoting its Windows 2000 software, which may also have cost tens of millions of dollars to develop. However, once it was developed, it cost only a couple of dollars per copy to record on a CD. There was an even greater economy of scale operating. These days of course it would only cost a few cents to allow the software to be downloaded.

If the Ford and Microsoft experiences were exceptional, then there might be some hope for the assumption that economies of scale are not important. However, obvious economies of scale operate in most manufacturing industries, and company managers routinely factor them into the calculation of production runs and product prices.

Moreover economies of scale are a lot more widespread than just in manufacturing industries. Economies of scale can also result when people learn from experience – the so-called learning curve effect – and that happens just about everywhere.

It's a surprisingly regular effect, first noticed on aircraft assembly lines: the time people take to complete a task drops by around 20% for each doubling of the total number of items produced. This creates an economy of scale because the biggest company, meaning the company making and selling items the quickest, learns faster, and its production costs decline faster than its competitors' as a result.

There have been many studies of learning curves by management consultants, and there is no industry in which the effect has been sought and not found[24]. Even in farming, which John Stuart Mill used to illustrate decreasing returns, industrial agribusiness is proving economies of scale can be found. The learning curve applies in both labour-intensive and capital-intensive industries. It has been found in an astonishing diversity of industries, a few examples being semiconductors, life-insurance, steel, beer, facial tissues, knit fabric, air travel, hydroelectric power and typesetting. It also seems to apply to all cost components of a business, including overhead, advertising, research, engineering, marketing, supplies purchasing and labour.

The pervasiveness of economies of scale has a simple and fundamental implication. The biggest firm can undercut its rivals and grow at their expense. It's a recipe for monopoly. Evidently it works, because today many industries are dominated globally by only a few companies. The only reason a company doesn't achieve complete monopoly is that there are usually some less profitable niche markets for smaller companies to occupy.

By the nineteen nineties only five firms accounted for more than fifty percent of worldwide business in each of the automobile, airline, aerospace, steel, electronic components, and electrical and electronics industries[25]. Ironically, some agricultural industries were even more concentrated, with three firms accounting for more than eighty percent of business in the marketing of bananas, cocoa and tea.

So you can see that economies of scale present another big problem for the neoclassical theory. If economies of scale are widespread, there's no guarantee that firms won't grow to dominate their market, and thereby cause market failure. If many major industries are in fact dominated by only a few firms, then market failure would seem to be the normal condition. This means markets do not yield optimal results.

Pervasive disequilibrium; competition eliminates competitors

We can look at this in another way, that even more directly undermines the neoclassical conception. During its growth phase, the bigger Ford's business got, the faster it grew. When the growth rate of something is proportional to its size, in other words when it grows by the same proportion or percentage every year, then its growth is exponential. The early phase of debt growth in Figure 3.3 is exponential, when debt increases by 15% per year.

Exponential growth is characterised by a doubling time. If the doubling time is five years, then after ten years it will have quadrupled. After fifteen years it will be eight times bigger. After twenty years, sixteen times bigger. After fifty years (ten doublings), it will be over 1000 times bigger. After one hundred years (twenty doublings), it will be over 1,000,000 times bigger. Yes, over one million times bigger. Exponential growth can result in enormous sizes after surprisingly short times.

Here is the key point: exponential growth is a signature of instability. While exponential growth is occurring, the system is out of balance. It is far from equilibrium. If economies of scale are pervasive, then new firms are bubbling up all the time, growing exponentially until they fill the available niche, keeping everything off balance, far from equilibrium.

Even if aggregate economic activity is fairly steady, in a modern economy there is a continual jostling of competing firms. There is certainly competition, but it does not yield a gentle, tidy, optimal equilibrium. Rather, competition eliminates competitors until there are only a few big ones left on the field. Then the whole field may be upended when a new technology appears and defines a new field of competition. The first entrants onto the new field typically gain an advantage from rapidly increasing economies of scale, and before long the new field is dominated by a few big boys.

Systems like this are known in modern fields of knowledge, like systems theory, physics, biology, and ecology. Such systems are called self-organising systems. Their behaviour can be quite complicated, and difficult or even impossible to predict. Their behaviour is radically different from the sedate general equilibrium of the neoclassical theory. We will explore self-organising systems more as we go along.

More sources of instability

Let's go back to that list of assumptions on which the neoclassical theory is based. We've looked in more detail at the assumption of no economies of scale and identified a fundamental problem. Not only are economies of scale widespread in modern economies, but they generate instabilities that will keep the economy well off balance, far from the putative general equilibrium.

Some of the other assumptions also are clearly unjustified. Unfortunately when they are made more realistic the result is also to predict instability instead of equilibrium. We have already been through one example.

For a market to function properly, everyone has to have reasonably complete information, and the information should be up to date. It is this information that enables the feedback that, ideally, would regulate the market and bring it into balance, supply equalling demand. In Figure 3.3, timely feedback brings debt into equilibrium, the supply of debt balancing the demand for debt. However if the feedback is delayed, debt overshoots, and swings above and below the level of balance. If the feedback is delayed too much, an overshoot and crash can result. The system is almost always far from equilibrium, and may never be able to stabilise at the equilibrium level. *Lesson: delaying market feedback can destabilise the system.*

A similar thing happens if information is not complete. Then the feedback is weak, and there can be an overshoot, followed by wild swings. Traders in international currency may trade a hundred million dollars in a morning's work. Managers of big financial funds may trade stocks worth tens of millions of dollars in a morning's work. There is no way at all these traders can have more than miniscule knowledge of the actual firms in the productive economy whose fates they are playing with.

At a more homely level, if you buy a small kitchen device from the supermarket, you do not thoroughly research its design and construction, to make sure it will perform as advertised for a reasonable time. No, you buy it in faith and ignorance, and it may fail within a week or a month. You'll be lucky if there's a guarantee, and if you can ever recover your money, because the manufacturer may be on the other side of the world. Or it may just not be worth your time to chase a refund.

It is absurd to assume that all transactions in a modern economy are backed by reasonably complete and timely information. The vast majority are not. The result is that financial markets can swing erratically and that good products can be displace by inferior products. *Lesson: incomplete information can result in instability, or highly sub-optimal results, or both.*

We could go on. Neoclassicists assume our transactions are not influence by third parties. Then there should be no fads and fashions, in which your teenage daughter desperately needs to dress like her peers, or you have to have the latest model car to maintain your social standing. Nor would there be herd behaviour in financial markets, in which traders notice everyone is buying so they buy, to avoid missing out. Or everyone is selling so they sell, to avoid being caught out. *Lesson: social interactions can and often do destabilise markets.*

We do not all have the same preferences. Neoclassical economists assume society can be reduce to the representative agent, which is the average of all of us. But if the local geek spends ten percent of his income on pizza, does Bill Gates spend ten percent of his income on pizza (even if he is still a geek at heart). If your teenage daughter spends every available cent on clothes, do you? If some of us are lenders and some are borrowers, do we all get wealthy at the same rate? Eggertsson and Krugman got new phenomena when they assumed two kinds of agent. *Lesson: differences in preferences can drive complicated economic behaviours that the representative agent assumption cannot capture.*

We cannot predict the future. Good heavens, we cannot predict the future even to the extent of listing the possibilities and their probabilities. The trouble is if we can't all predict the future even to that extent, then no-one has been able to show that the general equilibrium is possible, even if each of us has infinite computing power at our disposal. Oh dear. In fact, it has been shown in some interesting "games" that even when the future possibilities are quite limited our inability to predict the future can generate large and random fluctuations in supply lines[26].

The original neoclassical theory in effect considered only an instant of time, within which everyone weighs up everybody else's likely purchase price before actually making a purchase. This was mediated by the artifice of an imaginary auctioneer who kept calling for everyone's bid until everyone had taken account of everyone else's bid and no-one wanted to change their bid. Even neoclassical economists recognised this as an artifice. In effect the assumption suspends the flow of time. The assumption that we can all assign probabilities to future possibilities (called "rational expectations") was an attempt to allow time to flow without losing the general equilibrium. In effect this further artifice brought the future in from the great unknown.

However the future stays resolutely unknown. If the possibilities are unknown, there can be no proof of a general equilibrium. Physicists will recognise that the problem transforms from a closed, elliptical form to an open, hyperbolic form which is intrinsically evolving, each state depending on the system's past history. *Lesson: we cannot predict the future, therefore there is no guarantee of a general equilibrium.*

So we see that if you choose more realistic assumptions upon which to build a theory of economies, many of the alternatives imply instability: economies of scale, delayed feedback, weak feedback (e.g. from incomplete information), third-party interactions (e.g. social interactions, that can lead to fashion and herd behaviour in financial markets), multiple kinds of agents, and our inability to predict the future. This list is not complete, we'll encounter others as we go along. A system full of destabilising influences, and showing abundant evidence of instability, will not be at equilibrium. It may be far from equilibrium, all the time.

General lesson: we should forget about the general equilibrium and its putative optimality. There is no assurance free markets will bring the invisible hand to bear. They are just as likely, for all we know, to bring on the invisible foot. There is no basis, in theory or in practice, for believing free markets will yield desirable results. The neoliberal ideology has no basis.

A very different kind of system: self-organising complexity

If there is no general equilibrium, what is to be done? If economies are full of instabilities, do they just career randomly along? If that were true it might be hard to find any way to make sense of them, and to manage them. However the situation is probably not that bad.

The way forward is to recognise that systems with internal instabilities are *self-organising systems,* and there is a lot known about such systems[27]. An example of self-organisation in a modern economy would be the strong tendency of many market segments to become dominated by a handful of large firms. This imposes a recognisable structure within the economy: market segments with a few large firms, and progressively smaller firms filling progressively smaller niches. The economy tends to develop this kind of organisation spontaneously, under the action of its internal forces.

Another example would be the tendency, in many economies and societies, for wealth to become unevenly distributed, with a few people holding great wealth, many people holding little wealth, and a gradation in between, from larger numbers with little wealth through smaller numbers with more wealth. This is another kind of structure or order that is not imposed from outside: it develops from the internal interactions in the economy.

So there do seem to be some recognisable regularities within modern economies. They may or may not be desirable patterns, but they exist, so we can recognise the operation of *self-organisation* within modern economies. These examples suggest the plausibility of an idea that can be established more firmly with more exploration[10].

Self organisation is actually quite common in the natural world. We are more used to thinking of organisation being imposed by people, when we build things or arrange ourselves into organisations of many kinds. However once it is pointed out, it is easy to recognise self organisation in the world around us. Wind-driven waves on water, ripples on sand and patterns in clouds are examples. As wind blows over sand, any small bump in the sand tends to collect blowing grains of sand on its lee side, whereas grains tend to be swept up and over the windward side. The result is that a pattern of ripples grows across the surface of the sand. No external agent needs to plan it, it happens purely through the physical interactions between moving air and grains of sand. The air and sand self-organise, and the ripples emerge.

Emergence is a characteristic feature of self-organising systems. The internal structure *emerges* spontaneously from the internal interactions within the system. This is the source of the saying "the whole is greater than the sum of the parts". An *emergent property* or behaviour is one that can only exist when the full system is functioning – it cannot be seen in a single component.

A good illustration of emergence is a Mexican wave, popular with stadium crowds. When a Mexican wave comes around a stadium, your job is to sit until it arrives, stand or jump as it passes around you, and sit again once it has passed. The wave is simply the collective effect of everyone doing what you just did. You can't do a Mexican wave by yourself. It can only be done by a large crowd, which self-organises to produce the wave. Thus the whole (the crowd) can manifest a Mexican wave so it is, in that sense, greater than the sum of the parts (all the individual people), who can't do a wave by themselves.

Self-organising systems come in many varieties, some exhibiting quite simple patterns and others more complicated patterns. How complicated the patterns are depends, loosely, on how strong the internal interactions are. If the interactions are not very strong, the patterns might be fairly simple, like ripples on water or sand, or the oscillations of a pendulum (one of the simplest cases).

A system with strong interactions of the right kind can become very complicated. In fact it might be *chaotic*. A chaotic system fluctuates randomly. Its detailed behaviour cannot be predicted with any accuracy except for a short time (though its average properties might be fairly stable). Weather is chaotic, in this technical sense, which is why weather forecasts are only good out to about a week in advance.

Economies are probably not chaotic, because they do exhibit periods of relative calm. There might be a lot of jostling among firms going on, but the overall economy may be proceeding fairly steadily. Every now and then, however, a major change can sweep through an economy. This might be due to a market crash, or it might be due to a major new technology, like computers or the internet.

Systems with this kind of behaviour are called *complex self-organising systems,* or just *complex systems* for short. They arise when the internal interactions are not strong enough to generate chaos, but they are strong enough to drive complicated patterns. So just short of the threshold of chaos, at the edge of chaos, the behaviour is not chaotic, but neither is it simple or steady[28]. Rather, *complex* behaviour has a kind of shifting order. There are patterns but they don't persist. Small changes are happening all the time and every now and then there is a large change.

It seems that living systems operate in this edge-of-chaos borderland occupied by complex self-organising systems. I won't go into much detail about this, but it is of fundamental importance to the way we study living organisms and systems. Living systems must be studied as a whole, holistically, if their full behaviour is to be understood. If you dissect your frog, it is dead and won't croak or jump. Because economic systems contain living components (people, animals, crops, etc.) they also must be studied as a whole, not just as the sum of (highly simplified) parts in the way of the neoclassical theory.

The behaviour of complex systems could also be a description of our experience of life: a kind of shifting order, with small changes happening all the time and every now and then a large change. It could be a description of your own life, or of the history of nations.

Complex systems are more predictable than chaotic systems, but there is still an important aspect of unpredictability in their behaviour. When a big change does occur in a complex system, it may shift into a new state with recognisably different behaviour. During such a shift, the system is *hypersensitive* to slight disturbances. For this reason the outcome of the shift is not in practice predictable, even though the system is always deterministic. To predict the result of the shift, you would need complete and perfectly accurate information about the system just before the shift. We can never observe anything with perfect accuracy, so in practice we may not be able to tell what will happen.

Guiding the horses

So economies may not be chaotic, but if they are *complex*, then the job of understanding and managing them still sounds daunting. Again, there is a path forward, and it will not be too unfamiliar to the more pragmatically minded economic managers.

It is a matter of observation that markets are powerful. The operation of modern competitive markets provides strong incentives for firms to improve their product, to innovate, and to run more efficiently. Unfortunately in modern markets, as currently mismanaged, the invisible foot is as likely to operate as the invisible hand.

So, do we have to give up on markets and all become socialists? I don't think so. The problem is not markets *per se*, the problem is *unfettered* markets. The lesson is that markets should not be left to themselves. Rather, we should treat markets like *wild horses:* they are powerful, but they need to be tamed and guided if we want them to take us where we would like to go.

It may seem that not much can be said about managing economies if they are complex systems that are intrinsically unpredictable. However the unpredictability applies to the details of their behaviour. There is still much that can be said about the character of their behaviour. We are familiar, for example, with the dogness of dog behaviour, and we can readily distinguish it from the catness of cat behaviour. This is true even though we may not be able to predict, in a particular situation, if a threatened dog may grovel, or run away, or attack. There are still sensible ways to treat a dog, such as not threatening it, or if it feels threatened then not cornering it.

We need to get to know, as well as we can, the nature of the economic beast we are dealing with. Our goal is not to try to control the detailed behaviour of the economy, but to manage its overall trends and general character. For example, obvious present trends are to increase material throughput and to rapidly degrade the natural world, and we would be wise to reverse both of those trends. The character of the present economic regime is to be erratic and brutally indifferent to the fate of individuals, whereas an economy that is more stable and takes care of individuals as well as abstract aggregate measures would have a more benign character.

We can begin our reassessment of the nature of an economy with the recognition that an economy is not a piece of clockwork, it is a living system. As I have already noted, economies are embedded in human societies and an organic world, and so important parts of them are literally alive. Peoples' taste for fashion and the collapse of a soil's microbial ecosystem are just as much a part of an economy as factories and finance.

On top of the complex responses of their living components, modern economies have their own complicated internal feedbacks, some that tend to stabilise them (invisible hands) and some that tend to destabilise them (invisible feet). An example of instability is the runaway growth of a firm that gains a lead in economies of scale. It is the presence of strong internal feedbacks and resulting instabilities like these that generates the sometimes-erratic behaviour characteristic of complex systems. It is also the internal feedbacks that make economies tricky to manage, because their responses are hard to predict. We need to be cautious with our interventions, carefully monitoring their effects and being willing to back off and try a different approach. We certainly need to avoid claims of universal panaceas. We also need to restrain our politicians, who love to change things with gay abandon and with little effort to verify effects. They do this not only because of ideology, but also because politicians want to be seen to be fixing things.

Familiar tools, new context

Guiding markets is not a new idea, we have been doing it for a long time. There are two main traditional tools: rules and incentives. A third, reconnecting feedback pathways, will be introduced shortly. Incentives affect what is profitable and what is not. Where the profit is, markets will follow. So long as it is profitable to exploit people and trash the Earth, we can expect that people will be exploited and the Earth will be trashed. If we want that to change we must find ways to make it profitable to treat people and the Earth well. There is a long history of applying subsidies and taxes to influence what is profitable. Subsidies are positive incentives, whereas taxes are negative incentives. Market operation can also be changed through rules, usually referred to as regulation. This is a blunter instrument, but it also has a long history.

Incentives affect the feedbacks that operate within the economy, and feedbacks are what determine the character and behaviour of a complex self-organising system. When a market functions according to the neoclassical claim, our individual actions are collected through a stabilising (negative) feedback system and the collective result is a benign outcome – the invisible hand does its work and prices come to an equilibrium. However in some situations, as in an unregulated common or a falling market, our individual actions are collected through a destabilising (positive) feedback system and the result is not benign – the commons are eaten out, or the market crashes. The invisible foot takes over and there is a dramatic instability.

To give economists some credit, many have long recognised some examples of what they call market failure, and agreed that intervention is necessary to achieve a good result. A pertinent modern example is the destruction of natural habitat that supplies "ecosystem services" to people in such forms as clean air and water, a resilient natural world, potential medical cures and so on. The difficulty is that a firm that destroys habitat gains the profit, but does not have to bear the full costs, which are spread across the whole community. This is an example of the so-called *tragedy of the commons*. The solution proposed by economists is to impose a tax on such firms so the cost of their activity is "internalised", their prices reflect the real costs, and the market can then work properly.

Pollution is another case of market failure. Sir Nicholas Stern, reporting in early 2007 on the likely costs of avoiding global warming, called the pollution of Earth's atmosphere with carbon dioxide emissions "the greatest market failure in history". Really though, it is part of an even larger failure – the failure to protect the natural environment as a whole. Rather than pretending that bad outcomes are the exception, an "imperfection" in an otherwise orderly system, we must recognise that bad outcomes are common, or even these days the rule.

Another well-known example of market intervention is the progressive income tax, which intervenes retroactively in the labour market by taxing high-income earners at a much higher rate than low-income earners. Not all economists agree this intervention is justified, but many societies make the political decision to intervene, either because they think it yields a healthier and more cohesive society or because they consider it immoral not to help the less fortunate among us, or both.

However a better solution to extremes of income would be to address the problem closer to its source. To do this we need first to recognise there are artificial mechanisms that pump wealth from the poor and middle class to the rich, examples of which will be noted in this book. If we remove those mechanisms, or modify them, then we might achieve the result more efficiently and effectively. Poor people would be rewarded more in proportion to their contribution, rich people would have to pay more of the costs of production, incentives and costs would be better aligned with goals so markets would function more efficiently, and a costly tax bureaucracy could be reduced or eliminated.

The latter approach would be an example of redirecting the connections within the economic system so feedbacks flowed differently. This is a less recognised approach to economic management, but it can be a more effective way to shift the behaviour of the economy than just changing the strength of an existing feedback using incentives or regulations. It requires more creativity, and we will encounter some creative examples as we go along.

There may also be situations in which we choose to exclude markets. Natural monopolies, such as the distribution of water and electricity, used to be widely recognised as requiring a different form of management, run by or monitored by government. Privatisation under the neoliberal regime has generally resulted in poorer and often more expensive service, due to cost cutting and excessive share-holder profits. Perhaps the most spectacularly poor example was the privatisation of the California electricity market, which resulted in customers suffering brown-outs and losing billions of dollars, and the subsequent collapse of the principal corporate villain (Enron). Natural monopolies should be carefully considered individually to find workable arrangements.

If markets need to be managed, there is clearly a role for government. The government's role is to monitor the results of markets, to monitor our collective opinion as to what kind of society we want, and to design and adjust policies so markets will yield better results. Such results will need to be judged much more broadly than at present, according to the quality of society and quality of life we achieve, a subject taken up later.

In practical terms the changes required to manage markets sensibly are not so radical. The big changes are in the recognition of the beast we are dealing with and in the overall intention of our management. We need to run our economies without the fundamental misconception that markets can be left to run themselves, and we need to free the whole subject from the messianic ideologies with which it has been plagued for the past couple of centuries. Indeed the existence of those messianic movements is symptomatic of the lack of firm grounding of the discipline of economics, which is pre-scientific. We also need to abandon the implicit and insane goal of increasing material production without limit, and to manage instead for improved quality of life.

In other words the implication of the failure of the neoclassical paradigm is not that we need radically new kinds of policy instruments. Rather it is to remove a persistent objection to the kind of market intervention we have been doing anyway, but fitfully, incoherently and often counter-productively. With a clearer justification for intervention, and with a clear intention and a clearer political will, we are likely to manage more coherently and therefore more effectively.

This is not the place for a more detailed discussion of the many ways in which incentives need to be adjusted so as to produce more beneficial results. There are many perverse subsidies that need to be eliminated, there are many unintentional perverse incentives that can be reversed with creative adaptations, and there are ways in which market feedback can be made more effective. Alternative forms of ownership provide some powerful options, as we will see later. Some of these possibilities are discussed more in my earlier books: *Economia*[29] and *The Nature of the Beast*[10]. Others will be found in the excellent summary of "complexity economics" by Eric Beinhocker[26], and probably many other places. My objective here is to flag the existence of far more sensible ways in which markets can be structured and managed.

A more positive future?

This chapter has shown that the neoclassical conclusion, that the economy will come to a general equilibrium under the action of free markets, is an extremely contrived conclusion. Neoclassicists have struggled desperately to "save" the general equilibrium, but the quest is hopeless. Under real world conditions, there are many sources of instability that ensure modern economies are always far from equilibrium.

The implication for how we conceive economies is profound. The neoclassical view is that an economy is like a rocking chair or a rocking horse. If you tip it one way, it will spontaneously roll back and, if not perturbed any further, come to rest at its equilibrium position. On the other hand a more realistic evaluation of market mechanisms has shown that markets are more like wild horses. They are powerful and erratic, and need to be tamed, harnessed and guided if they are to be useful to us.

A complex self-organising system has *radically* different behaviour from a pendulum or a rocking horse. If we recognise the nature of the beast we are dealing with and address it appropriately, by learning its ways and working with its tendencies, then we are likely to find economies can be more benign and beneficial than we would have thought possible.

Although the behaviour of real economies is radically different from the neoclassical fantasy, the more pragmatic economic managers have necessarily recognised many of the real behaviours of economies, and acted accordingly. Most of the tools we need to tame and manage real economies are already in use, so the practical means of economic management will not be radically changed.

What *will* be different is the recognition that such management is necessary and natural. The chorus decrying any "interference" in the economy can be ignored. We can focus, undistracted and without regret or apology, on the task of learning the behaviours of economies, and on creative ways to manage them with the most elegant and effective interventions.

LEARNING TO SUBTRACT

Polluting for wealth and happiness

IF a chemical factory sells $3 million worth of chemicals in a year, but creates pollution that costs $1 million to clean up, then, in dollar terms, how much better off would you say we are? You would say, I expect, we are only $2 million better off. However economists and politicians say we are $4 million better off. Instead of *subtracting* the $1 million cleanup cost from the $3 million production, they *add* it.

Why do economists add a cost as though it is income? Because they rely on the Gross Domestic Product as a measure of wellbeing, and that is how you calculate a GDP. The GDP is essentially the sum of all those things we do that are bought and sold. It is the sum of all our activities that involve the exchange of money.

Calculating a quantity like GDP would not necessarily be much of a problem if the GDP were just an obscure thing used by economists to measure total economic activity, so long as they were clear that's all it is. The problem is the GDP has become the dominant measure of wellbeing. It is the goal of almost every government in the world to keep the GDP increasing. When the GDP increases, politicians and economists say "the economy has grown", and this is universally acknowledged, within mainstream political discussion, to be a good thing.

It is claimed that a growing GDP means we are becoming richer. It is assumed that if we are richer then our wellbeing is improved. Neither claim is necessarily correct. Over the past half century or so the GDP and wellbeing have become less clearly related. It is quite possible that GDP could increase while both wealth and wellbeing were static, or declining. Some argue that is already true.

There are in fact *several* fundamental problems with using GDP as a measure of overall wellbeing. One is that costs like pollution are added rather than being subtracted. Another is that many of our beneficial activities do not involve the exchange of money, so they are not taken account of. Another is that it is not a measure of wealth, it is a measure of income. Another is that it is a purely material measure. Another is that no account is taken of the state of our communities and society as a whole, nor is any account taken of the state of the Earth.

It is quite possible to use more sensible measures of our state of wellbeing, or even just of our material net incomes and wealth. Such measures have been developed and are being improved all the time. However they do not dominate the headlines the way "growth" (of the GDP) dominates the headlines.

The heavy reliance on GDP severely distorts our priorities, and our view of ourselves. Anything that falls outside the materialist and very blinkered purview of mainstream economics is regarded as secondary, irrelevant, or an expensive luxury to be attended to only as and when we become richer. As I will illustrate, that dismisses a mother's love, healthy families, healthy communities, a tolerant and safe society, and the health of the Earth, our sole and irreplaceable life support system.

It's all just activity

Why do economists *add* the cost of cleaning up pollution to the GDP? It is because the GDP is defined as the sum of all activities involving money, regardless of the desirability of those activities. It came to prominence during World War II in the USA. At that time the government was heavily involved in directing the economy to support the war effort. It might therefore have been presumed that most activities were contributing to the overall effort, and the GDP was helpful in informing the government on overall levels of production.

However once the war was over, what assurance was there that most activities were beneficial? Pollution was already an old phenomenon, associated especially with the industrial revolution. An even older problem is the presence of people who sell shonky goods, or who practice other kinds of fraud. Then there is the occurrence of accidents and disasters, and the necessity of maintenance and replacement of equipment and infrastructure.

A sensible way to deal with such problematic activities is to set up a balance sheet, like a shop-keeper, with income on one side and costs on the other. You then add up both sides, *subtract* costs from gross income, and arrive at net income, or profit.

One version of this approach is the Genuine Progress Indicator (initially known as the Index of Sustainable

Economic Welfare[30]). As an example, the calculation of the GPI for Australia in 1996 is shown in Table 4.1 below. We don't have to worry about the details here. The point is just to show it is possible to put gross income in one column, estimated costs in the other, and subtract costs from income. You will see that various kinds of pollution appear in the Debit column. There are also things related to the state of society (unemployment, crime) and other aspects of the environment. Commuting is considered a cost. Illness is a cost. Accidents are a cost.

Long ago Ralph Nader noted that every time there's a car crash the GDP goes up. A few years ago when bushfires raged into Canberra, then my home town, and destroyed about 500 houses, the local economy was boosted, according to economists. The cleanup of the huge oil spill resulting from the 1989 grounding of the oil tanker *Exxon Valdez* in Alaska noticeably increased the US GDP. This is the same nonsense as the chemical pollution example. Accidents, pollution and natural disasters make us worse off. We may have to work harder to repair the damage, and thus be more economically *active*, but that keeps us from doing more productive things, or from enjoying our lives.

So the first fundamental problem with the GDP is that just adding up activity takes no account of whether the activity is useful, useless, harmful, or repairing previous harm. To an economist it's all just *activity*.

Why did economists continue to use GDP as a measure of wellbeing, or at least of what used to be called *standard of living*? I make no claim to understand the minds of mainstream economists. My best guess is that it's because free markets are supposed to ensure that all activities are useful. During World War II, government direction was intended to play this role. After the war, the government withdrew from such direct central management, but markets are supposed to play the same role.

However this still doesn't explain why the cost of cleaning up pollution or repairing damage from accidents and natural disasters would be considered as contributing to the benefit of the economy. There seems to have been a failure to think carefully (or at all?) about how to do accounting in a national context.

Some economists may say, at this point, they *know* the GDP is only a measure of total activity, not a measure of quality of life, or even of net material benefit. It's not their fault if politicians mis-use the GDP. In fact the inventor of the GDP, Simon Kuznets, specifically warned that it should not be used as a measure of the quality of life of a nation.

However I haven't heard a sustained campaign by the economics profession to get the GDP replaced by a proper balance sheet, one that shows incomes and costs and calculates the *net* benefit of our activities. Using the GDP to measure our "standard of living" or national income violates the most elementary requirement of accounting – that costs are subtracted from gross income.

Unpaid activity – loving baby

A second fundamental problem is that the GDP doesn't count anything that does not involve money. Not everything we do deserves to be counted as contributing to national production, it's true. Playing in the back yard or attending a concert is how we enjoy our spare time, and does not contribute to national production. However growing vegetables in the back yard arguably does contribute, since it substitutes for something that would otherwise be bought, involve the exchange of money, and count towards both

GDP and GPI. Exactly which things ought to be counted may be debated, but what about volunteer work for charities, or raising children?

Marilyn Waring came up with the example of six mothers who stay at home caring for their babies[33]. The mothers' loving care doesn't register with the GDP, because they are not paid for it, so their loving care has no value according to our national accounting. However if each mother were to hire the next to baby-sit her child, then money would change hands and the GDP would go up.

Thus having someone else care for your baby is implicitly regarded as more valuable than caring for your own baby, in the sick world of our national accounting. Governments anxious to see the GDP rising have little incentive to encourage mothers to stay home and care for their babies. However governments have a real incentive to see mothers out working, because then their paid work and their child care costs add to the GDP.

This kind of problem is even more important in poorer countries, in which much more activity may be at the local village scale and fail to register in the GDP. This means, on the one hand, that some such countries may not be quite the 'basket cases' some economists describe them as. On the other hand if people are displaced into cities to work for a pittance as land is taken over for cash cropping, then the people have to pay for things they formerly did for themselves, or obtained from the local village. The shift from growing vegetables to buying fast food adds to the GDP and thus counts as progress, whereas it commonly represents a significant regression in the person's health and happiness, and in the health of the nation's social fabric.

Table 4.1 includes the item Household and Community Work in the Credit column. This is the estimated value of activity that contributes to national productivity but does not involve money, things like volunteer work for charities. It is a very large amount, 55% of Weighted Personal Consumption (basically everyone's personal monetary income), and over half of the net GPI. So this item seems to say that over half of Australians' net wellbeing came from unpaid activities in 1996.

There seems to be a rather dramatic implication here. It is that all of the frenetic activity of the monetary economy contributes only about half of our net wellbeing. Much of the total of productive and beneficial activities, monetary or not, is cancelled out by the negatives in the Debit column.

Australia's GDP for 1996 was $432 billion (in 1990 dollars). But according to Table 4.1 over 40% ($184 billion) of the activity that might have counted towards the GDP were actually costs that reduced our wellbeing.

Now the GPI includes some important items that are estimated with varying degrees of confidence, and it is appropriate to debate how such things should be counted. Therefore the specific numbers I have just noted should not be taken too literally. However the numbers certainly raise important issues. The most important issue is that the GDP may be extremely misleading, even as a measure of material standard of living.

One manifestation of this is that the relationships between GDP and wellbeing, and GDP and GPI, seem to have changed over time. In the post-war decades, until roughly 1970, most people would not have disputed that their wellbeing was rising along with material wealth and the GDP. Since then, many people are not so sure their wellbeing is really being served by a "growing economy". Figure 4.1 compares the changing GDP *per capita* (i.e. per person) with the GPI per capita for both Australia (left) and the US (right).

In both cases the GPI has risen by a smaller proportion than the GDP, even declining for a time in the US. In Australia

Table 4.1.Australian Genuine Progress Indicator, 1996[31,32]

Credit		Debit	
[Personal consumption]	[260.9]	Unemployment	19.76
[Income distribution index]	[107.87]	Underemployment	2.02
		Overwork	10.09
Weighted personal consumption	281.43	Private defensive expenditure (health and education)	12.19
Public cons. expenditure (non-defensive)	25.35	Commuting	5.44
Household and community work	155.08	Noise pollution	2.40
Services of public capital	6.09	Transport accidents	5.01
Net capital growth	5.87	Industrial accidents	7.63
		Irrigation water use	0.64
		Urban water pollution	3.58
		Air pollution	9.42
		Land degradation	4.51
		Loss of native forests	4.81
		Depletion of energy resources	42.59
		Climate change	22.90
		Ozone depletion	0.00
		Crime	9.94
		Net foreign lending	21.10
Total Credit	473.82	Total Debit	184.03
Net (Credit *minus* Debit)	**289.79**		

(Amounts in billions of 1990 Australian dollars. Income distribution is an index used to adjust personal consumption.)

GDP increased by about 2.9 times, whereas the GPI increased by only about 1.8 times. In the US GDP also increased by about 2.9 times, whereas GPI increased by only about 1.7 times. So GDP suggests we were three times better off in 2000 than in 1950, but GPI suggests we were less than twice as well off. If GPI is a better measure of quality of life than GDP, the implication in both cases is that since about 1970 growth in the GDP has not resulted in much improvement of quality of life.

As already noted, the precise value of the GPI is not to be taken as highly accurate. Yet it corroborates the qualitative evaluation of many that increasing monetary wealth is not yielding an unalloyed increase in wellbeing. For many people work hours have been increasing, the pace of life has become too stressful, the natural world they used to value is retreating, and they worry about the global threats of pollution and destruction of forests, soils, and habitat.

One measure of this disaffection is that remarkable numbers of people have stepped away from the dominant lifestyle. About a quarter of working Australians *downshifted* over the course of a decade. This means they voluntarily took a reduction in income so as to improve their quality of life[35]. Comparable numbers downshifted in the UK[36].

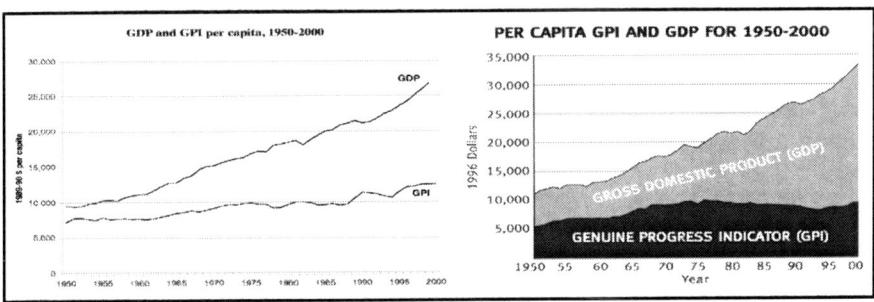

Figure 4.1. Comparison of GDP and GPI per capita over time for Australia (left)[32] and the United States (right)[34].

Quality of life?

These thoughts bring us to a third basic problem with GDP, its failure to take any account of the state of society. The difference between the GDP and GPI is not just because of more sensibly accounting for material problems, it is because the GPI also takes account of some social factors, including unemployment, underemployment, overwork, crime, and an adjustment for inequality (through the Income Distribution Index). Inequality has a significant effect not just on the quality of a society but even on economic performance[37]. More unequal societies are more conflicted, and income is not spent or invested as wisely as in more equal societies.

A striking portrayal of a dramatic increase in inequality in the US is shown on Figure 4.2, which was compiled by Robert Reich[38]. It compares the steady rise in productivity, 1947-2009, with the income of ordinary people. Productivity is the value of production per hour worked. Income closely followed rising productivity until the 1970s. After 1980 (the start of the Reagan years) there is a sharp break, and income rose by only 8% thereafter, compared with an 80% further rise in productivity. The reason, very clearly, is that most of the extra wealth generated in the neoliberal era has been creamed off by the very wealthy. That is shown explicitly in the lower part of Figure 4.2.

There are other social factors that make a difference to our quality of life. If work hours have increased, both because people work longer and because two adult partners of a household feel the need to work, then families are more stressed. Employment has become less secure, because neoliberals regard employees as just another disposable commodity, and that increases stress, along with unemployment. With greater inequality,

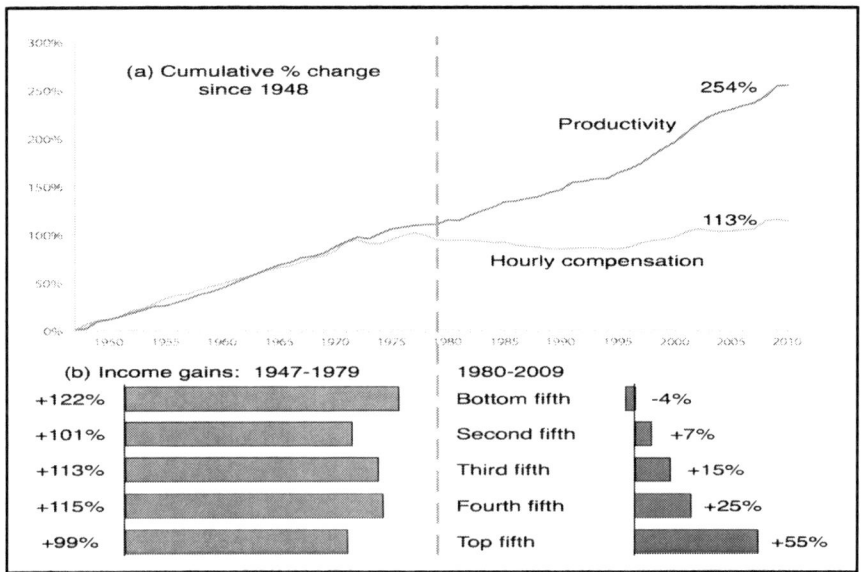

Figure 4.2. *The Great Regression of the neoliberal era, compared with the post-war Great Prosperity. From Reich*[38].

those at the bottom are more resentful, and that feeds into both ill health and crime. If people are working more, then they have less time for community activities, so they don't have as much social support as they used to, which compounds stress and ill health. Neoliberal hostility to governments, and particularly to social programs, has resulted in cuts to community and social services, along with infrastructure, so people receive less "in-kind" income and have less social support as stress levels rise.

Reducing life to numbers

A problem with both GDP and GPI is that they try to capture the state of society in a single number. At least the GPI tries to take some account of some social factors, but how do you compare the effects of crime or ill health with the value of a new car? In the GPI they are compared by using some documented costs of crime or ill health. But the negative effects of crime and ill health go well beyond their immediate cost. They raise personal angst and they may permanently reduce the quality of someone's life. On the other side, how to you value a mother's love for her baby? It is certainly extremely valuable, because the quality of our whole society is improved as we learn to raise children more lovingly and effectively[39]. There is no dollar measure of such qualitative things. So they are left out of the GPI, and the GDP.

The same thing can be said about the state of the Earth. You can put a dollar value on the timber in a forest, but you can't put a dollar value on the healthful and aesthetic experience of being in a mature forest, nor on its biodiversity, without which the Earth would be a less effective life support system. Nor can you put a dollar value on the medicines that might at some future time be discovered in plants that grow in the forest.

For these reasons an alternative approach called *Triple Bottom Line*, has been developed for measuring our overall wellbeing. It separately evaluates the economic, social and environmental areas. In this approach, some of the things in the GPI might be reassigned to other categories, or might appear in more than one category. Thus crime does involve financial costs that could be counted in the economic category, but it also indicates that a society is less cohesive and peaceful than it might be, so it would also appear in the social category, also as a negative. Similarly the loss of timber in a degraded forest would have an economic value, but a forest provides us with many other 'services' like clean water, better rainfall, a refuge for biodiversity, potential but undiscovered drugs and aesthetic and spiritual nurturing.

Thus the health of a forest might be listed in appropriate ways in all three categories.

There will be no 'best' way to summarise the wellbeing of a whole society, and many other variations and elaborations are possible. In a sensible world, the Triple Bottom Line would be better than the GPI, because it gives us more complete information with fewer debatable assumptions about whether things have dollar values.

However in the superficial and sensational world that passes for political discussion and reporting, politicians and media would rather reduce everything to a single number. Thus if the GPI were adopted as a primary measure we could expect it to be reported prominently, whereas a Triple Bottom Line might be relegated to page 6 of a newspaper, and might not appear at all in the infotainment that TV executives are pleased to call 'news'. For the time being, if we're stuck with a single number, the GPI is of some use, whereas the GDP is highly misleading and we'd be much better off without it.

It's worth saying a little more about GPI *versus* GDP. The GPI makes quite debatable assumptions, for example including a dollar measure of the negative effects of global warming (included through the euphemism "climate change"). I would agree with some critics that you could put almost any number for the "cost" of global warming. If it results in the collapse of global industrial systems, the loss of major agricultural production, epidemics, and flooding of half the world's cities and all of its harbours, what is the dollar cost, now? Others of course argue that such "alarming" possibilities are imaginary, but they are mostly not scientists with relevant knowledge. (Climate scientists are virtually unanimous, at the 97%+ level, that we do cause global warming and its effects may well be dire.)

So I agree the GPI is an approximate and imperfect measure. However I do not agree we should just leave important things out of our assessment of the state of our society. So the GPI is approximate and imperfect, but it is based in a sound approach, that we *add* benefits, *subtract* costs, and arrive at a *net* evaluation of our condition.

The GDP, on the other hand, is not based on a sound approach to evaluating the state of our society, even the material parts of our society the economics profession chooses to focus on. In no defensible form of accounting would you put all your transactions, incomes and costs alike, in the Credit column of a ledger, add them up, and proclaim that your shop is thriving because your Gross Shop Product is increasing. As a measure of our overall state of material wellbeing, the GDP is deluded and indefensible.

Distorted priorities

Using GDP to measure our wellbeing is not just a minor detail, it seriously distorts our society's priorities, as some of our examples illustrate. Consider the opening example of the polluting chemical company. Because the pollution reduces the GPI, a government anxious to keep the GPI increasing would have an immediate incentive to stop the chemical company from polluting. In the present situation, however, the $1 million cost of cleaning up the pollution is merely added into the GDP as 'activity', so the government has no incentive to stop the pollution. In fact the incentive is to allow the pollution to continue.

Similarly, unsustainable clear-cutting of Tasmanian forests would reduce the GPI but increase the GDP. Our crazy national accounting actually encourages governments to ignore over-exploitation of natural resources. In fact, since exploitation of resources and of people (through overwork and low wages) simultaneously increases corporate profits and the GDP, there is a clear incentive for an unholy alliance between unscrupulous corporations and unscrupulous or stupid governments.

What about the things GDP doesn't count? In Marilyn Waring's example of the mothers who stay at home to care for their babies, their loving care doesn't register with the GDP. However if each mother hires the next to baby-sit her child, then the GDP goes up. Governments anxious to see the GDP rising have little incentive to encourage mothers to stay home and care for their babies, but they have a real incentive to see mothers out working, because then their paid work and their child care costs add to the GDP.

We can now see that the familiar refrain "the economy is growing" carries a quite deceptive message. It doesn't mean what it seems to mean and it won't accomplish what it's supposed to accomplish. It doesn't mean our quality of life is improving. It doesn't even mean we're getting richer. It means we're busier. It means the dollar value of our paid activity is increasing, but it takes no account of whether that activity is useful, useless, harmful or attempting to repair some previous harm. It ignores unpaid activity and so undervalues or ignores and implicitly discourages many valuable things, including mothers' care of their children.

Even if we understand 'the economy is growing' to mean 'the GDP is increasing', unemployment and poverty will not be eliminated. They will, in the long run, still obstinately persist, as they have through decades of GDP growth. The factors controlling unemployment and poverty evidently must be found elsewhere.

Assessing wealth

One more problem remains to be discussed. The GPI is a balance sheet of income and costs. It is not a measure of our accumulated wealth. Despite the implicit assurance of polticians that we're getting richer, we don't actually calculate (or at least publicise) how rich we are.

Even if our net income is positive, that does not necessarily mean our wealth is increasing. This is because our wealth depends also on the value of any assets and liabilities we possess, and the values of assets can change. For example the price of housing has recently been falling in many countries, whereas the value of an oil reserve is increasing because the future supply of oil is believed to be limited. Then there is the whole question of depleting resources, both renewable and non-renewable. The GPI of Table 4.1 makes some attempt to account for the depletion of some resource assets, which is good, but there may be much more to be considered.

The Earth is being degraded rather rapidly. So long as there is no accounting of our assets (economic, social and environmental), then that degradation is invisible to our so-called national accounts. Politicians and CEOs can happily use up the Earth that we can then not pass to our children.

The Australian Government produces an annual State of the Environment report which, perhaps wisely, restricts itself to estimating whether various parts of the environment have improved or declined, without attempting to attribute dollar values. This is an imperfect exercise, since only some of many factors are considered, but it is commendable nevertheless, since it helps to keep the condition of the natural environment in the minds of our managers, however peripherally.

Even purely economic assets are not publicly accounted for. If they were, the level of private debt depicted in Figure 1.2 might have attracted some attention. Debt, of course, is a liability. With that much debt, we were not as rich as we might have thought.

Not even accounting

The problems outlined in this Chapter are of a quite different kind than those of previous Chapters. There is no arcane theory to be debated. There are no strange assumptions, or basic ignorance, about banking, money and debt and their potential effects on the dynamics of the economy. One might have thought the business of counting our income and wealth, at least in material terms, was fairly straightforward, at least conceptually, whatever the practical difficulties, and would be in basically reasonable shape.

However it is clear that even at the level of elementary accounting, mainstream economics is astonishingly deficient. Even to refer to "elementary accounting" is to understate the problem. Adding things that should be subtracted does not qualify as even the beginning of accounting.

I have no adjective to offer, to describe such a deficiency of thought. At the very least it involves a fundamental lack of attention to the task at hand. In addition, I have described current practice as highly misleading, highly distorting of our priorities, and highly distorting of our view of our present condition.

5

FINANCE: PARASITIC
AND DESTRUCTIVE

THE financial sector has come to dominate the major economies, and the financial centers at Wall Street and the so-called City of London are the largest centers of financial trading. The Wall Street financiers present themselves as a great boon to humanity, as essential to lubricating the economy, indeed as directly contributing a great deal of economic activity and wealth. They are so powerful they call themselves Masters of the Universe. This, apparently, gives them the right to ignore the law, to place their people in governments, and to buy themselves majorities in congresses and parliaments.

Hubris is one word to describe such attitudes, and it is a strong word, but I think the Yiddish word *chutzpah* does better. The best definition of chutzpah I have heard is the attitude of the man, on trial for murdering his parents, who begs for mercy because he is an orphan.

Perhaps I'm getting ahead of myself. Perhaps the present financial sector really is a boon to humanity, or at least a boon to economies, on balance. Mainstream economists certainly think so. The efficient market hypothesis, mentioned in Chapter 3, claims that financial markets correctly price entities and thus ensure capital is directed to its most efficient uses. This would be the lubricating role of finance. There is a little bit of truth to the claim, but we will see it is only a minor aspect of modern finance.

The mainstream claim can be challenged on different levels. One is whether the most profitable enterprises, to which financial markets may direct capital, are necessarily the most beneficial. A company promoting an improved computer technology may qualify. A company that has components made in a regimented sweat shop in India or China will not, because the power imbalance between poor foreign employees and a giant corporation mutes the feedback that might ensure employees receive fair compensation for their contribution (a topic we will return to later). The corporation may be escaping environmental regulations, as well as labour regulations, by shifting operations to a poor country. Without good market feedback, the invisible foot may replace the invisible hand.

A more telling question is how much of the activity on financial markets is even about allocating capital to the productive economy? Financial market bubbles are inflated by speculation. Speculators may not be concerned whether real-world enterprises are useful, or even profitable. They are often interested only in the financial market itself – will it keep rising or is it about to fall? Indeed when tens or hundreds of millions of dollars worth of stocks or currencies are traded within a few hours, traders cannot possibly know whether the real-world enterprises represented by financial instruments are useful, or even profitable.

I will show you shortly how this question can be fairly clearly answered, but first I will mention how some economists have debated it.

Conventional market critiques

The graph of the Dow-Jones index shown in Figure 3.1 fluctuates a lot, even apart from the big crash of 1987. To many people this "volatility" of financial markets looks suspicious. Should a well-functioning, "efficient" market be so volatile? Mainstream economists insist the markets are only responding to external stimuli, such as new information flowing into them, and that really they are just returning to equilibrium after being disturbed by such external influences.

The big drop of the 1987 crash cannot be explained as a response to external events. The change was only in the perceptions of market players. Therefore one must also question whether the smaller jumps are really due to external events.

Economists have tried using detailed statistical analyses to debate this question. Apologists claim traders' estimates of value tend to average out to the true value. However real-world markets do not fit this supposition. Detailed analyses have shown that market fluctuations are not the random walk apologists suppose, but consistently fit another kind of statistical distribution called *power-law*. Markets have a greater frequency of big jumps than is predicted by random walking, which is a sign of overshooting and overcorrecting[26]. The really big jump of the 1987 crash might then be just an unusually large fluctuation consistent with the power-law distribution, but it is quite inconsistent with the random walk assumption.

Other studies have shown that market value has deviated for long periods from what most economists would regard as good estimates of "true" value[26]. However such detailed studies depend on estimating "true" values, and the debates meander on.

You don't really need detailed analyses to demonstrate this point. The 1987 stock market crash changed the traders' collective estimates of value by around 30% globally within one day, even though nothing in the real world had changed significantly. The market price must have deviated from reasonable values before, or after, or both.

Apologists argue that active trading is required for prices to overcome "stickiness" and reach their true value. Stickiness just means the price might get stuck for a while on a value different from the "true" value because a large trader has posted a large order at a certain price. However their perception of stickiness is relative to the rapid fluctuations in the present market. With slower changes of market prices, trading would be correspondingly slower and no more sticky.

Frenetic markets

In the real sciences, a rough estimate addressing a key question sometimes yields more insight than fancy mathematical or statistical analyses. So another approach to this issue is to ask how much financial trading ought to be needed, to keep capital reasonably well allocated to productive enterprises? There are several ways one can attempt to answer this question.

A typical productive firm will survive for many years. Its fortunes may rise and fall in that time, but many firms are able to keep operating for quite long times. Some enterprises do not last long, and others last a very long time, but stock market investors interested in long-term returns will generally look for reasonably established firms to invest in. It is reasonable to suppose that the value of such a firm will change only moderately over the course of a year. Let us suppose, for the sake of this exercise, that the value changes by no more than 30%. Even if its price trend were consistently down, such a firm would take several years to seriously decline. So 30% seems like a reasonable upper limit, and many firms might change by rather less than this.

If you are an investor interested in long-term returns, and preferring also that your invested money allows the managers of firms to pursue at least a medium-term strategy to maximise the creation of wealth, then you might not want to trade more than 30% of your portfolio in a given year. If most investors pursued this strategy then the amount of stocks traded ought to be no more than about 30% of their total value. If the financial markets were mainly in the business of efficiently allocating capital, then most investors would indeed be pursuing just this kind of strategy.

So how much trading actually occurs in modern financial markets? When I first started to encounter this issue, I was reading William Greider's 1997 book *One World, Ready or Not*[25]. Even back then the numbers were striking.

The 1993 global rate of financial trading was equivalent to trading the entire annual output of the U.S. economy within four or five days. It was equivalent to trading the entire global stock of publicly traded financial assets every 24 days. Trade in U.S. government bonds turned over the equivalent of the entire U.S. Treasury debt in eight days.

Thus the world's stocks were turned over every 24 days, in contrast to our estimate that they would turn over only every few years. That's 24 days *versus*, let's say, 1200 days. Stocks were being traded about *50 times faster* than our estimate of how fast they might need to be traded.

The Sydney stock exchange is a small player in the global system, but in 1998 its turnover was over $A30 trillion, about $A17 trillion of this being in currency trade. The Australian Gross Domestic Product was then about $A450 billion. Thus the rate of trading was over 70 times the nominal rate at which wealth was being generated in Australia. The equivalent of the Australian GDP was being traded within about 5 days, consistent with the US estimate above. Even the rate of currency trading was nearly 40 times the rate of wealth generation. In fact the rate of trading in the Sydney stock exchange was equivalent to about half of the global rate of wealth generation.

A more recent estimate is that about $4 trillion a day is transacted in the global capital markets, according to the Bank for International Settlements. About four days' trade equates with US GDP for a year, and about two weeks' trade equates to the world's GDP.

These numbers are corroborated by a different approach, comparing present rates of trading with rates from earlier times, when finance was more regulated. In 1973, when the old Bretton Woods system of fixed exchange rates was abandoned, the turnover of the international currency markets was $10 billion to $20 billion a day. Two decades later the turnover was $1,200 billion a day, 60 to 120 times greater. Trade in goods and services had not increased proportionately. If financial trading had increased only in proportion to the real economy, Joel Kurtzman estimated that in 1993 $20 billion to $25 billion per day of financial trading would have sufficed to service real trade[40]. So trading was 50-60 times faster than Kurtzman's historically-based estimate of what was reasonably required.

These numbers consistently show that financial market trading occurs at a far greater rate than might be reasonably expected, and at a far greater rate than used to be the case before the deregulations of financial markets of the 1970s and 1980s. The difference is not ten percent or fifty percent. It is not even a factor of 2 or 3. *The difference is a factor of 50-100.*

If the difference were smaller, then you might argue these estimates are too rough, and you can't reach a trustworthy conclusion. But it doesn't matter if you say a reasonable rate of trading is 5% per year of 50% per year, you still conclude trading is much faster than required. Anyway the world got along with a much smaller rate of trading before 1973. And before some mainstream economist starts claiming markets were less efficient back then, let's remember that the post-war decades have not been matched for materially improving the lives of millions.

There is a simple implication of these numbers. *Only 1-2% of financial market trading is about the efficient allocation of investment.* The rest, 98-99%, is about something else. There is only one thing it can be about, and that is speculation. The vast majority of financial markets trades are about speculation. This was also the conclusion of Joel Kurtzman in 1993:

> Most of the [daily currency trade] goes for very short-term speculative investments – from a few hours to a few days to a maximum of a few weeks... . That money is mostly involved in nothing more than making money[40].

Strictly speaking, some of the trade is not speculation. *Arbitrage* is the practice of buying in one market and selling somewhere else at a higher price. Apologists argue, as usual, that this merely helps to bring the market closer to equilibrium. However as financial trading became computerised and markets interlinked electronically, price differences became smaller. Computerised trading therefore functions on millisecond timescales, looking for differences of small fractions of a percent. By trading very large amounts, the tiny margins can still yield large profits.

So arbitrage is not really speculation, it is more like the card game *snap* – the prize goes to whoever is quickest. However the reality is still that traders are creaming off huge amounts of money by playing games with the market. The tiny differences they play with have no serious significance to the real economy, so the claim arbitrage is making the market more efficient has no substance.

Parasitic, destabilising, inefficient

This information shows the behaviour of the financial markets in a quite different light, a light that admits a clear interpretation quite different from the mainstream economics story. It also exposes (again) the core of the neoliberal ideology as the bombast that it is.

The reason the markets fluctuate so rapidly and so much is because of their frenetic rate of trading, 50 times or more faster than is required. It is because huge amounts of money are being flushed around the world, tipping markets this way and back, in the quest for quick profits.

Far from bringing the markets to equilibrium, the speculative trading continuously destabilises the markets. Herds of traders rush this way and that, responding to every snippet of news, every rumour, every whim, dragging prices up, dropping them down, dragging them back up.

Rather than markets responding to external events, the markets are dominated by internal dynamics. Speculation exaggerates trends, pushing rising markets too high and then causing them to over-correct and fall too low.

Very large amounts of wealth are siphoned out of financial markets. According to a summary in mid-2011, US financial sector profits as a fraction of all corporate profits were, in 1995 34%, in 2001 46%, in 2006 41%, and in 2011 45%[41]. The Australian financial sector's profits as a share of GDP quadrupled since 1990[42], and currently it draws about one third of corporate profits. Evidently the financial sector is not a small part of the economy in either country.

Financial market apologists use such numbers to argue the financial sector is a large, vibrant and essential part of the economy. But most of the *activity* of financial markets is not useful. At best it is useless churning of money. We are back to the problem of using GDP to measure our wellbeing. It allows any kind of activity to be portrayed as socially beneficial. It allows financiers to parade the deceitful claim that they are making an important contribution to the world, even that they are generating huge amounts of wealth.

The truth is quite otherwise. At best, 98% of financial market activity is parasitic. It contributes nothing useful. It merely siphons money out of the productive economy and into the bank accounts of financial traders.

Worse, the rapid fluctuations generated by financial markets seriously impede the efficiency of the real economy. Managers of productive businesses routinely have to hedge against such things as sudden rises in the prices of inputs, changes in currency exchange rates, and sudden drops in their market capitalisation. Rather than managing for medium-term maximisation of wealth production, they must ensure large returns to shareholders on a quarterly basis so as to maintain stock prices. They must be more cautious in their strategy, they must avoid products that might generate high profits and benefits if there is too much risk involved.

The effects of market fluctuations on the real economy can be severe. William Greider quotes Kenichi Ohno of Tsukuba University speaking of the Japanese experience in the 1990s:

> A sharp appreciation of the home currency throws tradable industries into disarray. A sudden loss of international price competitiveness, amounting to 10-40 percent in real terms, is much larger than typical profit margins in these industries... . To survive, these industries are forced to make costly downsizing adjustments. These include operating below capacity, implementing cost-cutting measures, scaling down investment plans and even scrapping existing facilities, laying off workers ... outsourcing, shifting manufacturing bases abroad, joint ventures with foreigners, and so on.

Thus the disequilibrium and instability of the financial markets has reduced the productive efficiency of industry. It has also accelerated the globalisation of industry, by causing plants to be shifted abroad, and so magnified the problems associated with the export of jobs from the rich nations and the problems of instability, social disruption and exploitation in poorer nations.

Finally, every now and then the market fluctuations turn into a crash, and crashes are very destructive of the productive economy, and of people's livelihoods and lives.

Most financial market activities should not be described as investment. Real investment is the process of building new productive capacity, perhaps for a new technology. Real investment requires time for development, time for building and delays in reaping profits. Real investment cannot proceed if "investors" are fickle, and shift their money somewhere else without notice, but that is what financial markets currently promote. Real investment requires investors who have some commitment and patience, who are willing to defer their gratification, and who are willing to bear some risk that the new enterprise may not work out.

Put the speculators out of business

Since the GFC there has been talk of re-regulating financial markets, but the regulation usually discussed would only be marginal. It might return things to the 1990s and reduce some of the more egregious practices, but it would not come close to eliminating parasitic and destructive behaviour. Even so, regulation has been so resisted by the financial industry that little has actually been implemented.

Poorly conceived regulations can be onerous and ineffective. The most efficient and effective kind of intervention is one that changes the incentives in a market sector. There is one such policy that could rather directly eliminate much of the parasitism and instability from financial markets. It is to impose a small tax on all transactions. These are sometimes called Tobin taxes. The tax need be only large enough to take the profit out of short-term speculation and arbitraging.

The primary purpose of transaction taxes ought not to be to raise revenue but to slow and stabilise financial markets. A tax on stock transactions might be less than one percent, and on currency transactions it might be as small as 0.01%. Experience would be the guide to what the optimal level would be. The objective would be to bring the rates of trading down to reasonable levels, thereby damping short-term fluctuations and also reducing the parasitic creaming off of wealth.

There is a move, mainly in Europe, to impose so-called "Robin Hood" taxes on financial markets. Although these might be of some benefit, the name makes clear the intention is to raise revenue rather than the more fundamental goal of stabilising the markets. The movement is therefore vulnerable to the charges of promoting "wealth transfer" or "class war" rather than the more efficient and equitable operation of the economy. If the taxes are not large enough to take the profit out of undesirable market trading, then they will have little long-term effect, even though they might enable the funding of some compensation to the victims of market malfunctions. In other words they would apply band aids rather than healing the wound.

A further benefit of transaction taxes would follow if financial traders were forced to invest for more than a few hours, days or weeks, or milliseconds. They would then have to consider the actual productive potential of firms, instead of playing games with the wild fluctuations they themselves generate. In other words they would need to become actual investors, rather than speculators.

Managers of productive firms could then manage with longer term strategies than those focussed on next quarter's bottom line. Neither would they have to hedge against such large and frequent fluctuations of share capital and currency exchange rates. Thus the whole economy would function more efficiently.

If financial markets were reformed to the point where most of their activity was actual allocation of capital, rather than gaming, then the financial sector would be considerably smaller in terms of turnover, profit and "economic activity". As a rough estimate, based on the estimates above of a reasonable rate of trading, it seems the financial sector need not comprise more than a few percent of the economy. They might then be more focussed on providing a service, rather than holding the rest of the economy to ransom.

6

LAND IS NOT MANUFACTURED

Our Wealth

IF I have a shop on a roadside, and then you and Joe Blow open shops near mine, the value of my shop is increased because now people are more likely to stop, and more are likely to visit my shop. This will be more obvious if even more people build more shops, until there is a little shopping village that will be more likely to attract customers. However we can keep things simple and just think about three shops, because the principle still applies, even though the effect will not be as large.

Now, to whom does the *extra value* of my shop belong? To you and Joe Blow, or to me? Well why should you and Joe get the extra value? You already gained from joining the cluster. Your properties are worth more because of my shop, just as mine is worth more because of yours. On the other hand, I did nothing, and spent nothing, to create the extra value of my shop, so why should I get the windfall benefit?

The clue to solving this riddle is that each of us gains from the proximity of the others. The extra value comes from the *proximity* of our shops, not from any of the three shops individually. You and Joe could have built your shops separately in other places and none of us would get that extra benefit. If the extra value is because of our proximity, doesn't the value belong to us as a group? It is because we are a group that we each get extra value. You can say the extra value belongs to our little *community* of shops.

I will call this extra value the *emergent community value* – it emerges from the creation of the community, not from the individual investments made in the community. The name comes from modern systems theory, and we already encountered emergent properties in talking about self-organising systems. The presence of an emergent quantity is clear in this situation, it is a classic case of the whole being greater than the sum of the parts.

This idea of emergent community value has a long history. It is associated most with Henry George, who used different terminology and championed the idea about a century ago. George's best-known work is *Progress and Poverty*[43]. Followers of George more commonly refer to his concept as *social credit,* and various social credit movements and political parties have existed in various countries. George also used the term *incremental value.* Neither of these terms very clearly convey the essence and novelty of George's insight. The "Georgeist" message is also obscured by the insistence of George and many of his followers that a single tax, on land, can fund all government activity. That is a quite separate issue, as there is no necessary relationship between land values and the things we want government to do, and the claim only distracts from the key insight regarding emergent wealth.

The idea of emergent community wealth is not considered in modern mainstream economics and not recognised in policy. As a result the extra value emerging from the existence of a community can be captured by individuals. Out of that arises land speculation, property booms, skyrocketing land costs in city centers, perpetually overstressed public services like transport, increased inequality, and community priorities distorted to suit the interests of a wealthy few. That's quite a list of problems.

For example, in 1999 a new underground train line was built in London. The cost of the line was £3.5 billion, which was paid by taxpayers. However the emergent value accruing to properties within one kilometer of stations on the line was estimated to be £13 billion. Much of that property was owned by a relatively small number of landlords and developers, so they got the lion's share of the £13 billion in extra value. Because the project was financed by taxpayers, the net effect was to transfer both taxpayers' existing wealth plus a lot of the emergent public wealth to a few private entities, who scored a huge windfall without having to lift a finger or spend a penny[44].

The emergent value could instead have been used as collateral to borrow the cost of the project, which would thereby have been self-financing, requiring no input of taxpayers' money. The net emergent value of £9.5 billion could then have accrued to the communities along the line, and thence to all their residents, instead of to a few developers and landlords.

This suggests how emergent community wealth could be captured by the community and spent on community services. The community's worth would then actually increase more. We'll come back to that idea. In the meantime, because speculators can capture that wealth for themselves, everyone else is worse off.

Not just another commodity

Not only is the idea of emergent community wealth not used in mainstream economics, but when it is raised it is often dismissed out of hand as being a form of socialism, which it is not. This neglect reflects ignorance of the idea's history and of ideas emerging from modern systems theory, which gives the idea a more general foundation. The result of neglecting emergent wealth is a major form of wealth transfer, to the rich from everyone else, leaving many in our society to battle along with less than their share of the wealth. So why are so many economists so limited in their view of their subject?

One reason seems to be that land long since came to be treated as if were just another commodity. If there is a shortage of nails and the price of nails goes up as a result, this encourages an increase in the production of nails, until the shortage is overcome. The invisible hand does its work.

Similarly, goes the logic, if there is a shortage of land in a city, then the price will go up. People will be forced to build high-rise buildings that use less land, to compensate. So, in a way, the market generates a response to the shortage. But in the process an older couple might be priced out of their neighbourhood because of rising land taxes. On the other hand they might be able to sell their land for far more than they paid for it thirty years earlier and gain a windfall profit. This might generously fund their retirement, but the community they lived in will have been disrupted.

The trend to rising prices of land in the centers of cities certainly generates responses, but the responses are not necessarily equitable or efficient. Those who happen to own land that appreciates in value will gain a windfall profit. Speculators will move in and buy as much land as they can, so they can capture such windfalls for themselves. Both of these responses transfer unearned wealth. As we saw with the London underground example, that wealth must come from somewhere, and it may come from taxes on other people or from diverting wealth that properly belongs to the community.

If more land could be manufactured in the center of a city, then the market response would be more like the response to the shortage of nails. More land would be supplied until the shortage was overcome. At that point the price of land would presumably return to its pre-shortage level, determined by the cost of producing land rather than by the shortage. Of course this is a fantasy because we can't manufacture more land in a city center.

The point is that the market response to a shortage of land is very different from the market response to a shortage of nails. The failure of mainstream economics to attend to this difference is what leads to the long list of inequities listed earlier.

Reclaiming community wealth

Because land cannot be manufactured, it needs to be handled differently from nails. Central to this is to recognise the existence of emergent community wealth.

One of the ways a community could capture its emergent community value is to vest ownership of all land in a community land bank, with shares held by all residents in proportion to their investment in the community. That way the emergent value would flow directly to the community bank. Individuals would be allowed the right to use the community's land, and they could still own any improvement they made on the land. There would still be ample incentive for initiative and industry, but one source of unearned windfall would be removed.

Although emergent wealth is not recognised in mainstream economic theory, it is fairly widely recognised by local advocates and some local authorities. According to Alperovitz[45] there are many local land trusts in the US, and many local authorities that retain public ownership of land, and they use their ownership to capture emergent wealth for the benefit of the community.

This basic idea of a land trust has been creatively elaborated by Shann Turnbull[44]. He has proposed adaptations of existing contract and ownership arrangements that would enable a community to capture and retain its emergent wealth. He proposes separate titles to the land and the improvements, such as dwellings. The external value, the emergent wealth, would accrue to the land, and the land would be held by a Community Land Bank. Residents would receive shares in the CLB in proportion to the area of dwelling floorspace they owned. Absentee landlords and nonresident entities such as businesses and public agencies would not be entitled to any shares in the CLB, and thus would not own land, though they would be allowed to rent it. In this way the emergent wealth of the community would accrue to the CLB and through it to the residents. The equity thus gained by the CLB could be used to finance public infrastructure, as in the example of the underground London train line just discussed, rather than being drained off by local or distant speculators.

A further innovation proposed by Turnbull would be for developers' ownership to transfer progressively to the CLB and residents over the period in which the investment is depreciated for tax purposes. Such arrangements are used, for example, in Build, Own, Operate and Transfer (BOOT) infrastructure projects such as toll roads. The idea is that the investor garners the profit from operating the infrastructure for, say, 25 years, after which ownership transfers to the relevant government entity. The same principle could be applied to building a block of flats. In that case ownership of a flat would progressively transfer from the developer to a renter. Ownership of the land would be vested in the CLB, but the tenant would be progressively granted shares in the CLB in proportion to the fraction of the flat owned by the tenant. At the end of the contract period (say 25 years), the tenant would own the flat and the associated shares in the CLB.

Although developers under such a BOOT scheme would not have access to windfall profits from emergent wealth, which would be retained by a CLB, such investments could still be attractive because a developer would avoid the cost of purchasing the land, which is commonly comparable to the cost of a dwelling. Investors would consider such an investment viable because the depreciation period is the period over which expected income from the asset will ensure a profit. Of course a developer might also choose to sell immediately to any resident able to purchase the flat at the outset.

For residents unable to purchase immediately, such an arrangement would allow them to become eventual owners for no more outlay than a normal rent. This would overcome the common problem that renters just pour money down a hole and never have anything to show for it. It would make a big difference to the lives of the poor, because they would be on an up escalator, actually accruing wealth. (If it seems like they would be getting a free ride, we should remind ourselves that wealthy speculators ride up escalators all the time, leaving many of the rest of us trying to scramble up the down escalator.) Their wealth would come from two sources, the progressively increasing ownership of their dwelling, and their ownership of the associated shares in the CLB. The latter would be capturing the emergent wealth of the community, so their net worth would increase as the community increased in value.

An attempt was made to avoid land speculation on emergent community wealth in Canberra, the Australian national capital founded in 1927[46]. It was widely recognised that building a new city from nothing would cause large increases in land values, and initially there was enthusiasm to capture this value, and use it to fund the building of the city. Land tenure was leasehold rather than freehold, and lease prices were controlled. However several flaws in the design or implementation of the system led to its quick abandonment. At the beginning of the scheme it was decided land would not be re-valued for twenty years, so the emergent value that was supposed to be captured would not even be visible. Early in its operation, trading of leases was allowed, which got speculators back in business.

The most relevant factor for our discussion here was that large price differences developed between Canberra and the major cities, principally Sydney and Melbourne. This meant on the one hand that someone moving from Sydney got a windfall from selling in Sydney and buying in Canberra, and on the other hand that it was difficult to move from Canberra to a major city where prices were higher.

Had there been a community land bank, the appreciating value could have been captured for community members.

People moving away could have sold their shares in the CLB and retrieved the capital gain, to help pay the higher prices in other cities. People moving to Canberra would have been required to buy shares in the CLB, so they would pay for their share of community infrastructure, and gain no windfall.

7

WORKERS AND BOSSES UNITE!

Democracy itself will always be stunted by the exaggerated political power exercised by concentrated wealth. The problem is not that capital is privately owned, as Marx supposed. The problem is that most people don't own any.

– William Greider[25]

MAINSTREAM economics considers the distribution of wealth to be a matter for social decision, and not the business of economics. Supposedly, the way wealth is distributed requires subjective judgements about social arrangements, and economics is held to be an objective science that does not sully itself with such warm and fuzzy concerns. However much mainstream theorising is based on a supposedly representative agent, which excludes from the beginning the question of distribution of wealth, because all agents are implicitly the

117

same as the representative agent. To address differences in wealth, there would have to be differences among agents.

It is a common expression and a common perception that "the rich get richer". Some people add "and the poor get poorer". At a time when inequality of wealth has been clearly documented to be rapidly increasing, it is impossible to deny that the rich are getting richer faster than the poor might be getting richer. It is also possible to argue from the evidence that the poor are getting richer only very slowly, or not at all, or that some are even getting poorer. Are these claims true? If they are true, what would be causing wealth to flow disproportionately to the wealthy? Could it be to do with the way our economies are structured?

These are not small questions. William Greider's simple statement above identifies a central source of pathology in modern capitalism, a pathology that has provoked severe and prolonged social conflict. Much of the destructive conflict of the past century grew out of the tension between owners and employees, those who own capital and those who do not. That includes the communist revolutions and the consequent Cold War and nuclear confrontation, the major ideological division within the democracies, and the continuing contests within other societies between common people and ruling elites.

In fact it is not hard to identify mechanisms in our economies that tend to channel wealth to the already wealthy. The disparity in ownership of capital is one, though we must enquire further, as to how this disparity in ownership comes about. This chapter and the next will identify some of those mechanisms. This chapter focusses on kinds of ownership and how they affect flows of wealth. Other mechanisms affecting wealth distribution are implicit in other chapters. The main mechanisms identified will be summarised in Chapter 10.

Why does mainstream economics neglect this topic? At a minimum it reflects a monumental failure in curiosity, because disparities of wealth play such a central role in our societies. Plausibly, it reflects a blindness of an ideological kind, since there seems to be a strong self-selection among those entering mainstream economics to favour the prevailing capitalist paradigm. Regardless, we need to pursue this very neglected enquiry.

Industrial co-ops

Scattered through the towns among the mountains and valleys of northern Spain, in the Basque country (Euskadi), is a network of cooperatives. The cooperatives operate within carefully structured relationships, and are part of the Mondragón Corporación Cooperativa. The corporation was founded in the town of Mondragón in 1956 by graduates of a local technical college. Their first product was paraffin heaters. Currently it is the seventh largest Spanish company in terms of asset turnover and the leading business group in the Basque Country. In 2010, the Corporation posted total revenue of 14.8 billion euros, roughly 20 billion USD. At the end of 2011 it was providing employment for over 80,000 people working in 256 companies in four areas of activity: Finance, Industry, Retail and Knowledge[47].

The Mondragón cooperatives, in other words, are not just a collective of poor hippy basket weavers. They are big, modern, industrial business. Yet they operate in accordance with a Statement on Co-operative Identity that largely eliminates the perverse incentives that contribute to many problems of governance found in organisations with more traditional management structures.

119

Greider's insight, that most of us do not own much capital and so have to seek employment by those who do, points us to a key problem. The problem is that the interests of owners are not the same as the interests of employees. An owner's short-term interest is to maximise production and to minimise costs, including the costs of employees. An employee's interest is to work decent hours for a decent wage. At many times and places, these divergent interests have led to an extremely rich oligarchy or plutocracy and a vast majority of very poor workers.

In more enlightened times and places (unfortunately confined mainly to some twentieth century democracies), it has been recognised that an enterprise will do better if employees are healthy, and enthusiastic about their work. It is in the employees' interest that that the enterprise they work in is profitable and adaptable. However it has been remarkably uncommon that these more enlightened common interests have really been acted on.

There have been occasional enlightened employers who share some profits and some power with employees. In Australia, Fletcher Jones and Staff was renowned for decades for producing sturdy, high-quality clothing. In Britain, E. F. Schumacher[48] cited the example of the Scott Bader Company. The owner moved beyond sharing profits with employees by forming the Scott Bader Commonwealth in 1951. In the latter, employees became, collectively, full-fledged owners with rights and responsibilities in running the enterprise. Contrary to widespread predictions of doom, the enterprise continued to flourish in its new form, and flourishes still[49].

The intention of founder Scott Bader went beyond allowing employees to own some capital. They could, under conventional arrangements, have done that by buying shares in any company, though whether they could have afforded it is a different question. Rather, Bader questioned the need to divide people into owners and workers at all. In the new arrangement, employee-owners have rights and responsibilities. They have a right to some say in how the company is run. They then necessarily have responsibilities to make sensible decisions.

Employee-owners also operate under different incentives. The old conflicting and perverse incentives are removed. The employees' interest in the enterprise being profitable and adaptable is now explicit. The owners' interest in having healthy and enthusiastic employees is also explicit. (By the way, it is telling that we don't even have a word for *employee-owners*.)

Forms of collective ownership

The common form of collective ownership at present is the corporation, but this fails to resolve the conflicting incentives of bosses and workers. In fact it makes them worse, because shareholders can be so distanced from the operation of the business they may have little or no knowledge of conditions under which employees work, especially if the business is located overseas. The disconnection is worse again if shares are held through a large investment fund, such as a retirement fund. In that case owners commonly will not even know which companies they have a financial interest in.

Within the corporation, the hierarchical command-and-control system usually applies. The major problem with this is that information flows mainly down a hierarchy, and information flows upwards only very inefficiently, so that top executives will usually be ignorant of many practical problems that may exist within the operation, quite apart from the satisfaction or otherwise of employees.

Yet another problem with large corporations is that a third group, the managers, has its own incentives that coincide neither with those of distant owners nor those of subordinate employees. Outrageous executive salaries, even in failing companies, are only the most obvious symptom of this divergence of interests.

As well as the cooperatives already mentioned, other kinds of ownership exist that go some way to mitigating the conflicting incentives within large businesses. In the 1950s in the United States, the investment banker Louis O. Kelso invented the *employee-ownership trust* to allow employees to purchase their company[50]. In the United States such trusts are known as ESOPs, or "employee stock ownership plans".

Largely due the efforts of Kelso and his followers, about fifteen hundred American businesses now have majority ownership by employees through such trusts. Prominent examples are United Airlines and the Avis car rental company. Many others have lesser degrees of employee ownership[25]. The number is still only a small proportion of all firms, but the feasibility of employee ownership cannot be questioned – it exists in the heartland of capitalism.

It has been a widespread practice in Japan to offer a share of ownership to employees, and is an integral part of an understanding of mutual interest between employers and employees. Employees are encouraged by this structure and by explicit incentives to offer suggestions on how to improve operations, and to try new ways of working. Such inclusive attitudes on the part of management played a large role in the dramatic rise in the efficiency and quality of Japanese industry during the latter half of the twentieth century.

If employees own the company, then if they have a

problem with how much they're paid, or with workplace safety, or with how the company is run, they have the power to fix it. If owners have a problem with how much employees are paid, or with how hard they work, and the owners are also the employees, then it's their own problem. Owner-workers have to find their own balances among levels of pay, safety and maintenance costs, investment in the company's future, and so on. Those companies that cannot find workable balances do not survive. It is nobody else's problem. Strikes and lockouts are gone, the government does not need to adjudicate disputes, and its workplace regulation can be simplified just to ensuring some basic standards.

A likely reaction to such thoughts is that it could never work, but we have seen there are already many forms of employee ownership, even in the modern homeland of capitalism, the United States. It might be said that employees would not be capable of dealing with the tough decisions required to run a company. Certainly there would be difficulties of transition for a newly employee-owned company, and an employee-owned company would need to be innovative with its governance structure. Moreover United Airlines is owned by a syndicate of its pilots, admittedly not the entirety of its workforce, but it still embodies the alleged deficiencies of employee-ownership. It proves the viability of the model in a major corporation.

It might be said the economy would stagnate because the engine of capitalism is the capitalist's vision, ambition and control. However most large companies are collectively owned, and run by a professional management class, not by the owners. As well, small firms tend to be more innovative than large firms, and the large firms acquire innovations by buying the small firms. The claim that the economy would stagnate under more distributed ownership is thus simplistic and self-serving. There is still plenty of scope for creative and ambitious people under other forms of ownership, as publicly-owned corporations themselves demonstrate.

Employee-owned firms are also efficient. Many studies have shown they tend to be more profitable, more competitive and more efficient. This is especially so when people are actively trained in self-management. So the more employees not only own their firm but feel actively involved in running it the more productive the firm tends to be. This should not be a big surprise.[45]

Ownership, or at least a role in governance, can even be distributed beyond employees to other interested parties, or "stakeholders" in the ugly modern jargon. Mondragón provides an example, as we will see shortly. If a local factory is venting poisonous gases across the town and polluting the local water supply, and if townsfolk share ownership with employees, who are likely to be townsfolk themselves, then they can take direct action to fix the problem. (Nevertheless the government may still choose to retain an interest in pollution in order to protect children and other innocent parties.)

If suppliers feel they are being underpaid, unduly pressured by timelines, or threatened with arbitrary cut off, and they are brought into the governance of a company, then they have access to redressing their concerns. If Walmart's suppliers had a share of ownership they could end the exploitive stranglehold that Walmart exercises over them. Of course Walton family, that owns much of the company, might not prosper quite as much if it ceased to exploit its suppliers and employees – it currently holds as much wealth as the bottom 30% of US citizens[51]. However the fundamental market principle that producers pay full costs would be better served.

Working within communities; a cultural shift

Scott Bader's intention in forming his Commonwealth went well beyond resolving immediate conflicts of incentives. It was nothing less than to create a community within the enterprise, and to link this community to the larger community in which it operated. The former goal was facilitated by the new structure of collective ownership and responsibilities. Of course, for a community to come into existence, good will on the part of all those involved was also required. Evidently that goal has been attained to a considerable degree. The goal of linking into local communities was supported by requiring half the profit of the enterprise to be disbursed to local charities, and more substantially by instituting local councils in any community that hosted the company and its employees.

As Schumacher expressed it, the formation of the Scott Bader Commonwealth initiated a learning process for everyone involved. It has allowed them to go far beyond the tasks of making a living, of helping a business to make a profit, of acting in an economically rational manner. Beyond those mundanities, everyone has the opportunity to "raise themselves to a higher level of humanity", by participating in a supportive and creative community. They may do this, not just as a private pursuit that has nothing to do with the firm or its aims, but by freely joining in with the aims and activities of the organisation itself.

Daniel Quinn, author of the novel *Ishmael*[52] and two sequels, also champions the idea of combining community with making a living (in a short book with the magnificently subversive title *Beyond Civilization*[53]). His motivation is that our humanity is oppressed if we work in a vast system that benefits mainly Pharaohs (ancient or modern). We should return to doing meaningful and satisfying work, and we should do it within the small groups that our human nature is attuned to. We can no longer live as hunter-gatherer bands, nor in small villages (at least in the shorter term), so he advocates inventing modern analogues of such groups, that he calls tribes. He defines a tribe as a small community that makes its living together. Members of the community not only have a close social network, but they would also be dependent on each other to make their living together. His main modern example is of a circus troupe. Obviously this option is not open to most of us, he is just illustrating the idea. Rather, he says, we can use our imagination to find niches in the modern system through which a tribe can make its living. The Scott Bader Commonwealth and the Mondragón cooperatives come close to Quinn's conception.

The learning required to live and work in a community-cooperative involves a major shift of personal habits and expectations, and a major shift of organisational culture. The adversarial relationship, not just within work places but throughout modern industrial societies, especially in politics and law, is deeply entrenched. The routinely adversarial attitude of commercial media is another of the more obvious symptoms. As well, many people might at first be reluctant to become involved in governing, preferring to leave that responsibility to others as they have long been accustomed. It may therefore not be easy for these different forms of business (and life) organisations to spread and develop.

This is presumably one reason why cooperatives have not proliferated, but have remained a relative minority, despite their obvious advantages to most people, and despite some prominent and clearly viable examples. Another obvious reason is that in the conventional arrangement owners gain great benefits through their greater power, with which they are able to extract far more than their reasonable share of profits (as we will explore later). Cooperatives and other alternatives are routinely and contemptuously disparaged by neoliberals and the rich as backward and incapable of serving the needs of a modern industrial society. This is obviously untrue, but so long as the plebs are kept ignorant the lie can persist.

It is interesting and probably significant that the innovations we have looked at here come from groups with somewhat different cultures than mainstream Western society. I do not know much about Basque (*euskaldunak*) culture, but it may be significant that it survives as a minority group of moderately ancient lineage[54], a situation that would favour local cooperation in the face of outside pressure. Scott Bader was a Quaker, a group that practices respectful listening, self discipline and consensus decision-making, practices that are conducive to adapting to cooperative governance. As it turns out, the founder of sociocracy (below) was also Quaker.

Collective governance

Collectively-owned enterprises require more sophisticated governance systems than conventional businesses or corporations. The Scott Bader Commonwealth uses a number of cross-linking boards. The Commonwealth Board oversees both the business Company and a Charity Commission. The Company is overseen by a Group Board with links to management teams, a Members' Assembly and local community councils. The responsibilities of each board have been evolved in the light of experience, and they allow information to flow around the network to ensure the Commonwealth is abiding by its constitution, promoting its goals and meeting the needs of employees and local communities.

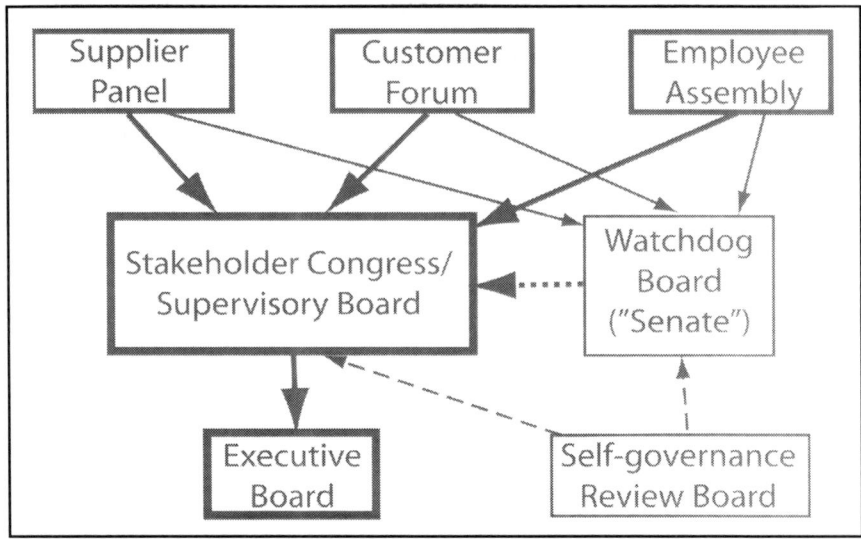

Figure 7.1. *Compound board structure suggested by Turnbull[55] for a cooperative or public-interest enterprise (with no shareholders). Solid arrows indicate election of representatives. Dashed arrows indicate appointment of chairperson only. Dotted arrow indicates appointment of a member.*

The Mondragón cooperatives also use a network of governing bodies, with complementary and cross-supervisory roles. Not only employee-owners are represented in the governance structure, but also suppliers and customers. The philosophy is that employees, suppliers and customers bring a great deal of valuable information to the business, and the main representative board provides a forum in which the different interests of the various groups can be worked through face to face.

Turnbull[55] has proposed a governance structure along these lines for a cooperative or public interest enterprise. For those of us who think better visually, it is illustrated in Figure. 7.1. This is not the place to discuss details of how such structures work, the point here is merely to open our minds to possibilities beyond the simple (and simplistic) hierarchies that dominate our world at present.

The Mondragón Cooperatives collectively have grown much larger than the Scott Bader Commonwealth or the single organisation for which Turnbull's compound board might be appropriate. Individual Mondragón cooperatives are deliberately limited in size to around a couple of hundred employees. If an operation grows larger than this it is split into two. In this way each workplace remains socially connected, in the important sense that everyone can have some real social contact with everyone else.

As the resulting network of cooperatives grew, two higher levels of organisation were developed. There are also cross-linking financing and monitoring bodies. The grouping has a network structure, and it is no coincidence that the whole network has grown in a way that closely mimics the organic world.

A yet more sophisticated governance system is *sociocracy*, developed principally by Kees Boeke and Gerard Endenburg in the Netherlands[56]. It draws on experience with industrial democracy and with Quaker Meeting practices, which demonstrate the value of self-discipline and respectful listening in meetings. It also draws explicitly on cybernetics, the science of control systems, which is used widely in engineering and computer science. Cybernetics is used in this case not to get everyone working with robotic efficiency, but to design a system that is robust in the face of peoples' quirkiness. In other words it helps to accommodate the essence of our humanity, not to ignore or obliterate it.

Sociocracy was refined in practice in Endenburg's company. It starts from the recognition that good governance does not just require decisions, it requires regular adaptation as circumstances evolve. Adaptation requires regular information about how current systems are functioning, how well tasks are being accomplished, and what new circumstances need to be accommodated. Governance is thus conceived as a repeating cycle of deciding, doing and monitoring, with the monitoring feeding back into new decisions.

A novel feature of sociocracy is that the different phases of governance are carried out in different organisational forms. Command hierarchies are not good for monitoring, because the flow of information up such a hierarchy is typically low. Lacking good information, the head of the hierarchy will not be able to maintain good leadership for long, so hierarchies do not yield healthy long-term leadership. However hierarchies are good for getting things done, so long as the task is clear and the people are in basic agreement with the need for the task. Therefore the doing phase of sociocratic governance is conducted in a command hierarchy.

On the other hand the monitoring and deciding functions of governance are conducted in a circular forum. The circles comprise a small number of people (from a few to a maximum of forty) who function as equals within the circle, though they may occupy different levels of the "doing" hierarchy. There may be many circles in a large organisation, and the role of each circle needs to be clearly specified. Once its role is defined, it is up to the circle to decide how it functions and what strategies it will use. It is responsible for monitoring within its defined realm, and for adjusting policy accordingly.

Each circle member has an equal voice in decisions. Decisions are by consent, which means that a decision is agreed when no-one has an overriding objection. Objections must be supported by a rational argument, but if a valid objection is made the circle goes into problem-solving mode to find a way around the problem. An example might be that a key person or machine does not have the capacity to perform the required function. The advantages of the circle process are that the relevant knowledge, experience and creativity of its members are brought to bear, that potential practical difficulties are more likely to be identified before they become problems, and that decisions have the consent of everyone who will be involved in carrying out tasks in the "doing" hierarchy.

Except for small organisations, there will be a hierarchy of circles. However the relationship between circles is designed to promote the flow of information both down and up. The higher circle chooses the functional leader of the lower circle (this is the person who will head the "doing" hierarchy), and that person's role in the circle is to convey the requirements of the higher circle to the lower circle. The lower circle selects a representative to participate in the higher circle. That person's role is to convey feedback to the higher circle, and they are full participants in that circle, not just messengers.

Even further – a fuller democracy

Sociocracy has a couple of intriguing and quite novel features that may not be immediately obvious. It forces us to rethink some of our usual concepts.

The first feature is that leadership is distributed. The organisation does not depend on one (allegedly) super-talented individual. Rather the organisation cultivates leadership in every one of its members. The organisation is self-organising, within the sociocratic architectural stencil, and self-directing.

The second feature is that, in effect, democracy is merged directly into governance, where it can operate as an intrinsic part of governance, instead of just occasionally and indirectly influencing governance.

If a political sociocracy were to be created, there would be no role for political parties. A major advantage would be the elimination of the unproductive adversarial contest between political groups. The whole point is to resolve differences as they arise and where they are most relevant, face to face instead of impersonally with strangers. The role of abstract philosophies would also be greatly diminished.

8

THE CAPITALIST MYTH

We know best, you're here to serve

ACCORDING to the capitalist myth all progress is dependent on capitalists. They are the ones with the drive and initiative to conceive grand schemes. They accumulate the money needed to build the factories to make the things we all want. They provide the jobs that allow us to live, and to make the money to buy the stuff coming from the capitalists' factories. Without them we would stagnate, and our societies would collapse into anarchy.

All despots, monarchs and pharaohs throughout recorded history have peddled this story. They are the ones who maintain order, who keep the barbarians at bay, who ensure we can rest secure in our modest existence that the world will be safe for us tomorrow – even if we are left cold and hungry by the king's tax collectors.

The present version of the myth is that the *current form* of financial markets is essential, and that it plays a real, positive and important role in the global economy. Wall Street spokespeople, some of whom are in the Obama Administration, are happy to promote these myths. Not only are minimal regulations routinely opposed, but alleged widespread fraud and other forms of criminality have never been seriously investigated. Much of the US Congress is beholden to Wall Street for campaign funds, and/or afraid that if they don't toe the line they will be opposed by a well-funded opponent in their next election campaign. At least the nineteenth century capitalists were dealing mainly in real productive enterprises like railways and steel. The modern masters of the universe mainly shuffle pieces of paper and computer entries, and claim those activities will put groceries on our tables.

A key underpinning of the current regime is the neoclassical claim that free markets are best. The rich and powerful are of course happy to support the mainstream economics profession in peddling this myth, because it allows them to become richer and more powerful.

The strategy of neoliberals in the US since Reagan took office has been to cut taxes on the rich, then use the resulting government deficit as an excuse to cut social services, which mainly benefit the poor and middle class. Supposedly, the economy will boom without the dead weight of taxes, and everyone will end up better off as the wealth trickles down from the wealthy. A similar story was peddled during the laissez-faire age of US capitalism around the end of the 19th century. The route to dominance in those days was different, a main one being the exploitation of outdated ownership rules to gain dominance in new industries including transport and municipal services. Another difference was that most people were already poor.

134

One source of belief in the capitalist myth is the writing of Ayn Rand, whose novel *Atlas Shrugged* is a favourite of US "neoconservatives". It portrays a strike by industrialists, scientists and artists, and the subsequent decline of the rest of US society. The obvious and fundamental flaw in this argument is that if *any* segment of society withdrew its services then the rest of society would suffer. That is the point of labour strikes. If doctors or judges or farmers went on strike, society would also suffer. The functioning of a modern society requires the collaboration of many parties.

Although they are associated, the capitalist myth is not the same thing as neoclassical economics. In fact, strictly speaking, they are incompatible. The neoclassical theory claims markets will always be competitive and no firms will be large enough to distort the market. Capitalists, on the other hand, have routinely grown their firms until a few of them dominate markets. These contradictions have not stopped the two getting into bed as the neoliberal ideology.

Neither is modern capitalism about accumulating capital (money) and re-investing it. Modern corporate big business is about borrowing (and claiming tax deductions) and repaying. And big modern corporations are not particularly innovative. They suffer from many of the same problems, due to size, that government enterprises are accused of.

The capitalist myth is nonsense. All enterprises in modern economies are collaborative in one way or another, and the bosses and money men are not the sole source of initiative and innovation. The periods of least restrained capitalism over the past century have not been the most prosperous, even in aggregate let alone for the poor and middle class, and they have generated the two greatest economic malfunctions of modern times.

If we dispense with the myth, then we can look more carefully at the contributions from people in various roles within modern economies, consider how rewards might flow more proportionately to their contributions, and find structures that more effectively apportion the wealth. We might also ensure responsibilities are less evaded. Directing the flows of wealth at their source is a more effective remedy for the capitalist pathology than devices like progressive income tax, which only retroactively redistributes wealth and which is prone to abuse through the creation of tax loopholes.

Plutocracy doesn't work

For the industrial nations the decades after World War II, until the early 1970s, were the most prosperous of the past century, by conventional economic measures. Furthermore that prosperity was distributed far more equitably than before or since. Table 8.1 summarises these measures for Australia and for the OECD (Organisation for Economic Cooperation and Development, basically the industrialised nations) up until 1993.

The three decades or so after World War II featured rapid growth of Australian GDP (over 5% per annum), relatively low inflation (3.3%), very low unemployment (1.3 percent!) and relatively low foreign debt (measured through the Current Account Deficit, which takes into account flows of money as well as the trade balance: 2.4% of GDP). During the decade 1974-1883 industrial economies were disrupted by a debt bubble, due to mismanagement of the Vietnam war effort, and "oil shocks", when oil supply countries raised the price of oil many-fold. Things settled down after that, but up to 1993 the figures were still not as good as those for pre-1974: growth 3.4%, inflation over 5%, unemployment over 8% and foreign debt over 4% of GDP.

Since 1993, GDP growth has been in the 3-4% range and inflation in the 2-3% range, but unemployment has only recently fallen below 5% and the current account deficit is over 6% of GDP. Thus the Australian economy has still not been doing as well as it did in the nineteen fifties and sixties.

A similar story can be seen in Table 8.1 for the whole OECD. During 1983-93 annual GDP growth was 2.8%, compared with 4.9% post-war. Inflation was 6.8% compared with 4.5% earlier, and unemployment was 8.4% compared with 3.2% earlier.

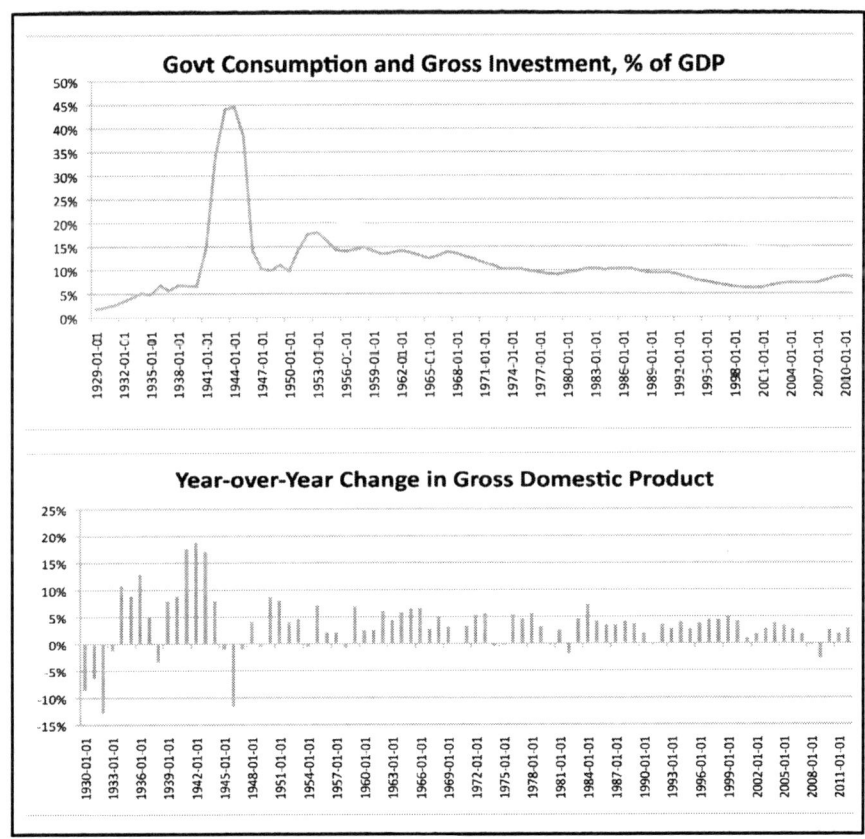

Figure 8.1. Top: US government spending, excluding "transfer" payments, as a percentage of GDP. Bottom: annual change in "real" GDP, i.e. with inflation factored out. From Dan Kervick[58].

Thus by economists' standard measures, including GDP growth, free-market economies have not done nearly as well as they did in the post-war era of managed economies. Before about 1980, most governments were much more involved in the economy, partly because the philosophy then was closer to that advocated by Keynes, who had argued that economies would run better if they were actively managed. Governments also worked more actively to counteract mal-distributions of wealth, through progressive taxes and by providing social services, and they invested directly in infrastructure and even to some extent in production of goods and services.

A clear measure of the change in government involvement in the US economy is shown in Figure 8.1. The top graph shows how government investment in the economy changed between 1929 and 2010. (The graph excludes what are called *transfer payments*, such as welfare payments, which do not directly change the total investment in the economy very much, they mainly shift who does the spending.) There was a huge surge of government spending during World War II, reaching nearly 45% of the GDP. In the post-war decades spending fell to around 15% of GDP, but this was still very much higher than pre-war spending: although depression-era spending had risen dramatically, the rise was from only around 2% to 6%.

So government spending was sustained at relatively high levels, around 15% of GDP, through the prosperous nineteen fifties and sixties. There was then a steady decline to around 10% of GDP through the seventies, arrested, ironically, by the Reagan administration. Another decline occurred through the nineties took spending as low as 6% of GDP, before another rise that still has not reached 10% of GDP.

The changes in GDP growth follow these spending changes in broad outline, as can be seen in the lower panel of

Figure 8.1. The US GDP grew hugely through the war, and continued strong growth through the fifties and sixties, after a brief post-war dip. Since then GDP growth has tailed off, consistent with the OECD averages in Table 8.1.

The US was finally lifted out of the Great Depression by the concerted action of everyone contributing to the war effort, with the government playing a major role in both planning and spending. There was a concern that the economy might drop back into depression after the war[59], but this was avoided by continuing strong leadership and spending by the government, and by the general confidence and "can-do" attitude of the population. This was the era of big government projects, like the interstate highway system and space exploration. In the neoliberal era, since 1980, both government spending and leadership have fallen away, and so has GDP growth. Such new wealth as has been generated, or extracted, has flowed mainly to the rich. Morale among the poor and middle classes is now very low, and common purpose has been lost.

Table 8.1 Economic performance, pre-1974 and post-1974.[57]

	Pre 1974	1974-83	1983-93
Australia			
GDP annual growth (from 1960), %	5.2	1.8	3.4
Inflation (CPI annual increase, from 1953), %	3.3	11.4	5.6
Unemployment (from 1953), %	1.3	5.6	8.4
Current Account Deficit (%GDP, from 1959), %	2.4	3.1	4.4
OECD			
GDP annual growth (from 1960), %	4.9	1.6	2.8
Inflation (CPI annual increase, from 1960), %	4.5	11.1	6.8
Unemployment (from 1953), %	3.2	6.4	8.4

The pattern evident for the US and the OECD applies more widely. Table 8.2 gives a more globally comprehensive summary of GDP growth than Table 8.1, and spanning more recent times. It also paints a very clear picture. Averaged over many countries, growth in gross domestic product (GDP) since the neoliberal ascendancy began in 1980 has been less that half what it was before. From 1960 to 1980, the average annual growth of GDP for 109 countries was about 2.5 per cent. From 1980 until 2005 the average growth rate for 175 countries was only about 1.1 per cent.

Table 8.2 includes a breakdown by income category, from the poorest to the richest, and only in the poorest category is there a slight increase from the earlier to the later period. It turns out that's because this category

Table 8.2 World economic performance, before and during the neoliberal era.[60]

Income range, US$	1960-1980		1980-2005	
	Number of countries	Annual GDP growth rate, %	Number of countries	Annual GDP growth rate, %
355-1225	29	1.7	28	1.8
1238-2332	27	2.4	30	0.7
2364-4031	24	2.6	33	1.0
4086-8977	17	3.6	40	1.3
9012-43713	12	2.6	44	1.3
Average	(109)	2.47	(175)	1.09

Each row shows results for a subgroup of countries defined by an income range. For example in the period 1960-1980 29 countries had average annual *per capita* incomes that fell between $355 and $1225; this defines the poorest group of countries. The bottom line shows growth rates averaged over all countries. Because of changes in availability of data, the particular countries falling in a given group may differ between the earlier and the later period.

includes India and China, which have not run neoliberal-style economies for most of this period. If they are excluded there's a slight decrease in growth rate for that group too.

For the second-poorest group, defined by incomes between $1238 and $2332, the change has been particularly disastrous, the growth rate falling from 2.4 per cent to 0.7 per cent. With the earlier growth rate they would have doubled their wealth in about 30 years, but with the actual later growth rate their wealth would take 100 years to double. At the average 1.09 per cent growth rate of all countries for the later period, wealth would take about 64 years to double.

The neoliberal era has also been particularly bad for Latin America[60]. Whereas Latin America grew by 80 per cent in the earlier two-decade period, it grew by only 11 per cent in the next two decades and a further 3 per cent from 2000 to 2005. If Brazil had continued to grow at its earlier rate it would have had European-level incomes today, and Mexico would have been not far behind. Instead Brazil in 2000 teetered on the brink of an economic collapse, and Argentina did collapse in 2001. The 1980-2005 period has been the worst in modern Latin American history, worse even than the Great Depression.

The contrast documented in Table 8.2 is all the more remarkable because the earlier period, 1960-1980, includes the difficult 1970s period of oil embargoes and an inflationary burst due to the Vietnam War.

These numbers show clearly that modern neoliberal capitalism has not delivered on its promise, even when only average and aggregate measures are used. If the distribution of income within countries is considered, then the failure is even clearer. Figure 4.2 showed that in the US wages, which comprise the main income of poor and middle class people, have been almost stagnant since 1980. The extra wealth generated since then has been creamed off by the wealthy. There has been very little "trickle down". Nearly 40% of that new wealth has gone just to those with the top 1% of incomes[61].

Thus capitalism, in its modern neoliberal form, is about the rich getting richer, and the rest can take their chances. This is nothing new. During the first great capitalist binge, a century ago, a few hundred US families accumulated fabulous wealth, easily comparable to the old monarchs of Europe, while most people endured grinding poverty. It took half a century of political struggle to achieve a reasonable share of wealth flowing to the poor and middle class[59].

Why plutocracy doesn't work

The mediocre performance of the neoliberal era should not be a surprise. The so-called "trickle down" effect is widely recognised to be without any base in real experience. The common people in the 1890s and 1920s certainly knew they were not becoming prosperous. The common people of Europe and the US knew they were gaining only slowly, or slowly losing ground, before the GFC.

As well as that, we now have modern studies, from no less an authority than the International Monetary Fund, showing that inequality retards economic growth[37]. The social effects of inequality are also now documented clearly[62]. People's self esteem is reduced if they feel they have inferior social standing, and this has many negative effects on their behaviour and health. People tend to be healthier and happier with the same absolute level of material wealth if they live in a more equal society.

The effect of inequality is not just psychological, although that aspect is very important.[63] Inequality and competitiveness can interact to create a downward spiral, in which, for example, the wealthier put their children in expensive private schools, while public schools are left underfunded and deprived of many of the better-prepared students. Wealthier people vote for government services and tax policies focussed on them, and services for the poor decline, so the poor and lower middle class receive fewer benefits from government services. In these and many other ways the poor are poorer not just in income, but also in public services, life skills, opportunities, self confidence and expectations, and so the gap between rich and poor widens.

This trend is clear in Australia over the past two or three decades, a major change for a society that has traditionally championed "a fair go for everyone". The United States, always a much less equal society, shows the results of such trends – impoverished ghettos and wealthy gated ghettos, with radically different life expectations and expectancies for their children. The subtitle of Stanley et al.'s book *Children of the Luck Country?* is "How Australian society has turned its back on children, and why they matter."[63] We need to be reminded why our children matter? That our societies could be so uncaring about or oblivious to the prospects of many of their children is a profound commentary on the state of their social and moral fabrics.

We should not need such studies to persuade us. Viewing the issue in these terms already concedes that we need to justify a less iniquitous society. My contention is that the purpose of an economy is to support everyone in sufficiency and dignity. The poorer people in a society are always looked down upon by the wealthier, so a highly unequal society does not provide everyone with dignity. Rather than having to justify this, it is up to those who magnify inequality to demonstrate they are not harming the less well off. Beyond a moderate range of inequality, the above studies show this is not possible.

Even if we consider only economic performance, there are clear arguments that have been made and forgotten. We need to remember them. In 1946 prominent Madison Avenue ad man Chester Bowles offered accessible arguments for a more equitable distribution of wealth than had prevailed in the US in the previous half century. In his book *Tomorrow Without Fear*[64], Bowles offered a simple example. If 1% of the population received 95% of the national income, with the rest going to everyone else, then the rich would never be able to consume the things the 99% poor majority would be capable of producing, and everyone else would be too poor to buy the things they produced. Lacking demand, production would fall and unemployment would leap. The rich would have no incentive to re-open or build factories with their wealth, so they would put it into speculation. The speculation would further destabilise the economy, as it had in 1929.

The effects of the inequitable distribution of income in the 1890-1940 period were close in kind to what Bowles described: grinding poverty and unemployment alongside extreme wealth, leading ultimately to a financial and economic crash.

Henry Ford offered his workers $5 a day because he recognised the people needed to be able to afford what they produced. His motives were probably not pure, because it turned out there were many restrictions on who got the $5 a day, and he was probably also forestalling the growing power of the labour unions.[59] Nevertheless he acknowledged the legitimacy of the proposition.

It was widely recognised at that time, even among prominent businessmen, that if the appeal of communism and socialism were to be muted, then capitalism had to do better by ordinary people. Many also recognised that high inequity slowed and destabilised the economy. Another of those who argued eloquently for the equitable distribution of wealth was influential attorney and banker Randolph Paul in 1947 in his book *Taxation for Prosperity*[65].

As noted in the previous chapter, mainstream economics considers the distribution of income to be a matter for social decision and none of its business, as it makes no difference, in their models based on *the representative agent*, who spends the money. Once again mainstream economics is shown to be deficient and misleading.

Of course the mediocre aggregate performance documented above is not the worst of it. The neoliberal deregulation of markets, particularly of financial markets, precipitated the Global Financial Crisis, which started the Great Recession that still continues for much of the world. The global financial system would have collapsed completely had it not been bailed out with huge injections of other peoples' money, and with new money created out of nothing. The global economy would have been thrown into deep depression had not some Keynesian-type government interventions kept it from sinking as far as it might have. Even so the periphery of Europe *is* in depression, thanks to the stupidity of neoliberal European central bankers, who repeat the mistakes that deepened and prolonged the 1930s depression. They make those mistakes for the same ultimate reason too: they are fixated on saving the rich from themselves, and the poor must go begging.

The earlier period of unfettered capitalism also led directly to the Great Depression. The super-wealthy accumulated so much money they could not spend it all on useful things, so they speculated. That speculation drove the debt bubble and crash that precipitated the depression in 1929. The depression was prolonged by the same problem: the super-rich were not spending their money, and they fought bitter political battles to prevent it being significantly taxed, or passed as wages to people who would spend it, even through the depths of the depression and into World War II[59].

So yes, the capitalist myth is nonsense. Unbridled capitalism simply allows the rich to capture more and more of society's wealth, through their economic power and then by corrupting politics and subverting democracy. It is particularly ironic that the most virulent modern form of capitalism has bred in the United States, which fought its Revolutionary War to free its citizens from the burden and oppression of the unearned wealth and privilege of Europe's monarchs. US capitalists have betrayed the Revolution twice over. Perhaps they should be called on their subversion and betrayals.

How should rewards and responsibilities flow?

The alternative forms of ownership surveyed in the previous chapter show that alternatives to old capitalism or modern corporatism are available and viable. Ownership by employees gives rise to a quite different flow of wealth, to all who share ownership. The flow can be much more equitable, according to contribution, and the degree of equity can be decided by the collective ownership.

Employee-owners are also less likely to evade responsibilities. They will obviously take care of the enterprise's responsibility to its employees, but the broader social connections among them may also foster a greater concern for other responsibilities, such as to the local community and to the Earth. Additional components in a governing structure can make the discharge of such responsibilities explicit, such as having suppliers' and customers' fora that participate in governance.

All of this raises some basic questions. What is an appropriate distribution of wealth? What factors or considerations might determine how to divide the wealth among those who contribute to its creation? Are there some enterprises that ought to keep all of their wealth, for example not even paying taxes, as some libertarians might argue?

To properly consider how rewards and responsibilities might flow, we need to think about the various roles people, firms and societies play in "economic activity". Contributions also vary by economic context, such as routine activity *versus* innovation.

Because human beings are social, we do many things collectively. Indeed our complex modern societies link us all in many ways. Very little of what we do could be done without the rest of society functioning around us. So to what extent are our "individual" efforts really individual? If our efforts are not really individual, then how are the rewards of our individual-plus-collective effort to be shared?

Essentially all economic activity in a modern society is collaborative. Even when an enterprise has a single owner and no employees, as in a small business or a family farm, its productivity is greatly enhanced by infrastructure and services provided by government. Transport and communications are obviously important, but so to are the legal system, a currency system, the education and research systems, and so on. We all inherit a great body of knowledge and technologies, which education makes available. Without effective government there would not be the social stability that is a precondition for a basic level of trust, and trust is necessary for the operation of contracts and payment procedures. Thus the government, as the agent of society, can sensibly be seen as a partner in every enterprise.

It follows that every enterprise ought to contribute financially to support the government. Normally this is done through taxes. There can certainly be a debate about the level of government services and functions, and about the efficiency with which they are carried out. However the systematic denigration of government by neoliberals is unreasoning and counter-productive, as the hollowing out of the US economy shows.

There can also be a debate about how to levy taxes. The experience of the past century carries the clear lesson that the burden should fall more heavily on the wealthy. This is not just a matter of morality and equity, it is necessary in order to keep a society and its economy stable and viable, as Chester Bowles argued nearly seventy years ago.

Turning now to enterprises with more than one participant, neoliberals might be dismayed to learn that their putative hero Adam Smith had a distinctly non-neoliberal view of how the flow of rewards in a collective enterprise should be determined. Smith considered that when collective effort is involved there is no objective way to separate the relative contributions of bosses, workers and machines. It is thus, in his view, a *social* choice as to how the rewards are apportioned. Smith concluded that wages are determined not by market forces but by the bargaining power of the employee. Even more dismayingly, Smith argued that the relative bargaining power of employers and employees was strongly influenced by laws the government passed and that, as a rule, the government sided with employers against employees[66].

There are many kinds of enterprises, and many kinds of roles within them. We don't need a comprehensive analysis here, just a general indication of the kinds of roles and what levels of rewards they might attract.

For the routine activity of established firms, a typical arrangement is that there are owners, management and workers. Typically workers get the least reward, management gets more and owners get the most. Some of these differences usually reflect different levels of skill or responsibility. Thus a skilled worker, a trained accountant or a manager responsible for million-dollar turnovers are paid more. In conventional firms, some of the differences in reward also reflect the imbalance of power between owners and employees. Owners have the most power, managers less, and workers the least.

In a cooperative it would be possible for everyone to share wealth equally, but there is still a case for some differences based on skills and responsibilities. In the examples of Mondragón and Scott Bader this is recognised, but there is a limit placed on the range of incomes allowed, such that the highest income will not be more than perhaps five or ten times the lowest salary. This kind of distribution of rewards would already make an enormous difference to most people in industrial societies, especially the anglophone countries.

If innovation is a significant part of a firm's activity, as it may be for a newly-established firm and will be for a firm developing a new technology, then there are additional roles to consider. Inventors are supposed to be rewarded through the patent system, but there are many kinds and degrees of innovation. For example employees may make valuable suggestions on how the work more efficiently, or how to improve a product, and they ought to receive an appropriate reward. Wise management will recognise and reward these roles.

If the firm has shareholders they, as owners, will of course get some a share of the wealth produced. Anyone who invests *savings* in an enterprise deserves a proportion of profits, because they could have used their savings for some other profitable activity. They should also be required to bear an appropriate share of risk.

The general question of how to finance an operation needs thorough re-examination. In pre-WWII capitalism, the capitalist provided much of the financing and demanded much of the resulting output. Our present financial system still tends to maximise benefit and minimise risk for investors. For example it exaggerates the power, and profit, of shareholders by permitting extremely short-term "investment", thereby facilitating parasitic speculation. It also ensures that the most exploitative firms world-wide set the level of returns expected by everyone, and that level of return will be disproportionate in most other less exploitative and less risky enterprises.

If an operation is financed by a new bank loan, then the bank will have created new money out of nothing. This is quite different from someone who invests savings, and ought to be treated quite differently. This topic will be taken up in a later chapter that looks into how money may be created and how investment may be separated from that process.

This brief discussion will be by no means complete, but it identifies some of the common roles in common situations. Identification of the contributions from each role is the starting point for considering how rewards and responsibilities might flow to participants.

The importance of being Owner

In modern societies rewards still flow mainly to those who own, as William Greider implied. Ownership, in turn, is assigned mainly to those who supply money, as distinct from talent or labour, so rewards flow mainly to the wealthy.

The result, as Greider lamented, is concentrated wealth and exaggerated political power.

The rhetoric of the more zealous advocates of private property and private enterprise may make it sound as though ownership is a fixed and absolute state, giving the owner of something the right to do anything he likes with it. However the rights of ownership are never absolute, because at a minimum there will be laws restricting the impact of the property's use on others, and there may be taxes to be paid. Nevertheless it is true that ownership is a foundation stone upon which the rules of wealth distribution are built.

However ownership is nothing more than a social agreement or convention. Many forms of ownership are possible, total or partial, individual or collective, unrestricted or conditional. It is for us to decide. Moreover many forms of ownership are already widely used. The forms of ownership we choose have a great influence on the characters of our economies and societies.

With ownership should also come responsibility. You should ensure that your cow does not eat your neighbour's vegetable patch. You should ensure that your chemical factory does not poison the river. Since you have sole control, you also bear responsibility. In a small society social pressure accomplishes much of the inducement to responsibility.

However large societies present many opportunities to avoid responsibility. You can survive for a long time in a large society by selling shonky goods to people you will never see again, but you could not do that in a village. We have many laws and regulations to try to hold people responsible, but it is always a competition between those seeking to avoid regulations and those seeking to revise and enforce regulations. Lately the avoiders have been doing better than usual. In fact one description of the modern corporation is "organised irresponsibility"[67].

Ownership might imply *full rights* of use or only *limited rights*. Thus you might own a farm, and your tenure would commonly be called freehold. On the other hand you might own the right to graze a piece of land without owning the land, and your tenure might be called leasehold.

Ownership might imply a *whole* or only a *part*. Thus you might own only a piece or *share* of an enterprise, rather than a whole enterprise.

Ownership might involve *minimal conditions,* or explicit *limitations,* or explicit *privileges*. Thus shared ownership might come with conditions, or it might be granted privileges, such as limited liability. In pre-Civil War America, the granting of limited liability often involved explicit restrictions, such as limits on capitalisation or the duration of incorporation. You might own a block of flats and the land it occupies, and you can then collect rents from the flats for as long as you own them, as well as capturing windfall appreciation of the block's value. On the other hand you might build a toll road at your own expense but own only the right to collect tolls over a twenty-year period, after which full ownership passes to the state.

Each of these possibilities is or has been commonplace in some places and times. Thus although ownership seems like a simple concept, the flexibility with which it can be applied allows us to have a great deal of discretion in its implementation, and thus over the flows of rewards and responsibilities.

Mainstream thinking, such as it is, is dominated by only two or three forms of ownership – individual private ownership, government ownership, and collective private ownership through corporations. Government ownership is a major issue for neoliberals, because they believe government is generally bad. However we have already mentioned straightforward reasons why it is sensible for government to be involved in many activities. The problems with corporate ownership that were noted earlier seem to be of little concern to neoclassical economists, though they are of concern to some marginalised schools such as institutional economics.

Mention of government ownership brings up socialism, which means government ownership of enterprises or activities. In most countries the government owns some key activities, such as public utilities (water, electricity and so on) or some parts of transportation or communications. So most countries have an economy that is to some degree "mixed", meaning a mixture of government ownership and private ownership. Over the past few decades many activities have been privatised, particularly in the Anglophone countries, but still some government ownership remains.

In some countries, or at some times, the government has owned other things, like airlines, a bank, mines and other key activities. In a fully socialist society the government would own most enterprises. In the communist countries socialism was combined with autocratic or totalitarian government. That form of socialism generally did not work very well, for the fairly obvious reason that decision-makers are too removed from the activities they are managing, so they have poor information and feel little responsibility for the consequences of their decisions.

Of course most corporations are run autocratically, and some of them are extremely large. The result is that their decision-makers are very removed from the activities they are managing, so they have poor information and feel little responsibility for the consequences of their decisions.

Anyway autocracy is not a necessary condition for socialism. The Scandinavian countries became fairly strongly socialist while remaining fully democratic, and their form of socialism worked quite well.

So socialism means government ownership, and it is rather common and not sinister. In cases of natural monopolies or key activities like courts and the military, governments are commonly and sensibly involved. Whether they are involved in a wider range of activities is something that ought to be debated case-by-case, without unhelpful ideological baggage getting in the way.

About 25% of electricity in the US is generated by about 2000 publicly owned or cooperative utilities. Customers of private utilities on average pay about 14% more than customers of these public utilities. Private utilities have to cover exorbitant salaries for their executives, as well as dividends to share holders. On the other hand public utilities typically pay much more reasonable executive salaries and return higher dividends to their communities. In many smaller communities income from public utilities is an important source of local government income, and many public utilities are taking the lead in promoting green energy sources. Public enterprises in the US take many other forms as well, from land trusts and public transport operators to deliverers of social services, hospitals, even hotels and convention centers.[45]

Even very large public (socialist) enterprises can do well. Prior to Margaret Thatcher's gutting of the British public sector, productivity growth in British nationalised mining, utility, transportation and communication companies consistently outpaced that of similar privately owned industries in the US[45,68]. That is just in terms of economists' usual narrow definition of efficiency too. Typically overlooked in standard analyses are externalised costs that the whole of society must bear. The US private health system is famous for its cost (about double that in other industrial countries) and for consistently inferior health in the US in general. How about banks? Could publicly owned banks cost more than the many trillions of dollars and the many livelihoods destroyed in the Global Financial Crisis and its continuing aftermath?

By the way this book does not advocate socialism as a general solution. When we understand the real nature of markets, based on what we can see rather than on the abstract neoclassical theory described in Chapter 3, it becomes clear there are many ways in which a market economy might be organised. The pathologies of corporate capitalism can be more effectively dealt with by careful structuring and management of markets. This means we might have a predominantly market economy, but one that works much more efficiently, humanely and sustainably than today's economies. This will be explored more in a later chapter.

Ownership by employees, on the other hand, is quite different from socialism. If employees own a small factory then there is no large, distant bureaucracy involved. They are the workers and they are the bosses, and they have both the benefit and the responsibility of running the show. The Mondragón Cooperative network is one of the most interesting and successful examples, and it shows clearly that ownership by employees is quite viable in the modern global industrial economy.

One way in which ownership affects the flow of rewards is exemplified by the capitalism of the nineteenth century US, in which a few people came to own and control a great deal of productive capacity. They lived lavish lifestyles, quite comparable to those of European monarchs, and paid their employees a pittance, so poverty was widespread.[59]

It may seem the corporate capitalism of the present spreads the wealth a little more widely, to shareholders and managers. However wealth is still very unequally distributed, because share ownership is mainly the province of the rich, according to the Economic Policy Institute's *State of Working America 2011*[69]. In 2007 in the US, the top 1% of shareholders held about 38% of share value, the top 10% held over 80% of the value. The bottom 60% held only 2.5% of the value. On top of that, the manipulations of financial markets described in an earlier chapter have again generated highly unequal wealth in the neoliberal era.

The bulk of the populations of the industrial nations are not in such dire poverty as their forebears were a century ago, but that is not due to the largesse of modern capitalists. Rather, it is due to the intervention of governments, under pressure from majorities of their citizens[59]. Nevertheless the US, still the richest nation on Earth, does have many people in poverty. It has the distinction of having *working homeless* – people who are employed, but paid so little they cannot afford a home. The concentrated ownership of corporate capitalism still results in a highly unequal and unreasonable flow of wealth.

Cooperatives commonly choose to allow significant differentials in wages paid to people in different roles, but the range tends to be limited to within a factor of ten or less, whereas in the corporate world ranges of factors of hundreds are not uncommon. Cooperatives also allow the issue to be debated and agreed upon, whereas the corporate world functions much more by internal dictatorship.

156

From Can-do to Won't-do

It is symptomatic of neoliberalism that the pervasiveness of collaborative enterprise, and of cooperation more generally, would be overlooked by neoliberals. Society is a cooperative undertaking. The continued success of society requires many complementary roles to be carried out. Society is the expression of our social nature. Individuals of social species trade some of their independence for the larger benefits of being part of a group. That is as true of a modern industrial society as it is of a band of early humans on the African savannah. It is the resulting interplay between our need for some autonomy to develop our uniqueness, on the one hand, and our psychological and physical need for social relationships, on the other, that gives life its richness. The neoliberal vision of society is impoverished, and its prescription for a minimalist government comes close to anarchy.

Unfortunately it seems to escape President Obama, and most of those called *liberal* in the US (meaning socially progressive), that the mission of the so-called neoconservatives (really radicals) who now dominate the Republican Party is to destroy all government activities other than the legal system (as pertaining to property) and the war-making capacity. That is the libertarian vision. This means not only ending or privatising the social security system, it means no government spending on schools, hospitals, roads, bridges and all other basic services and infrastructure, which is why bridges are falling down.

The result is that the US is being rapidly hollowed out. The nation that proudly built the interstate highway system is now letting it decay away. The nation whose government-sponsored science not only put men on the Moon but promoted the development of computers, the internet, and

157

many other modern technologies is now walking away from any such ambitions. The *can-do* nation is becoming the *won't-do* nation. US society, as a result, is becoming impoverished and embittered, and is increasingly turning in on itself in violence and scapegoating.

Other countries are not as far along that path, but the dominance of the neoliberal ideology means we *are* on that path, and the US shows us what to expect – if we have the will to open our eyes and see what is before us.

9

INSULATING MAIN STREET FROM WALL STREET

MONEY is perhaps the most powerful agent in our economies and also the object of great confusion. Money involves debt, and therefore it carries risk. In our present system the supply of money occurs through the issuing of bank loans, and this magnifies the risk involved in both functions. The entanglement with loans means we must also reconsider investment. There is thus more to be said on the subjects of money, investment, debt and risk.

These topics were foreshadowed in Chapter 2, where I also noted the way we supply money is not really a respectable topic. However it is essential that it be brought out into the light and discussed, because the monetary system we have at present is a powerful destabiliser of economies and is highly susceptible to extortionate manipulation. It is thus, directly and indirectly, another major distorter of the flows of wealth, strongly favouring the wealthy. If we want any hope of creating stable, equitable and enduring economies we must attend to the way we supply money and to how we invest in new enterprises. Mainstream economics is, yet again, seriously deficient in a central aspect of economies.

What is money?

First we need to figure out what actually money is. You will hear money described as a unit of account, a store of value, a commodity and a medium of exchange. Briefly, the unit of account role is trivial; the money we use at present is not a store of value, it is only a token of value; it is not just any commodity, it is a contract; and it is a medium of exchange. Here's how we can sort these things out.

The fundamental act of economic activity is exchange. If Jane is good at raising pigs and Tom is good at growing wheat, then they might each specialise in what they're good at and then exchange a pig for some wheat. They could do this without the use of money. In other words they could barter. This simple example illustrates the point of all economic exchange, which is to increase value. Jane could grow her own wheat, and Tom could raise his own pigs, but they work more efficiently if they each do what they're good at and then exchange. Being able to exchange gives them more value for the work they invest.

To put it another way, Jane and Tom gain more value if they specialise and then exchange. This is a founding principle of economics, famously expounded by Adam Smith. The story of the industrial revolution, and of civilisation, is as much a

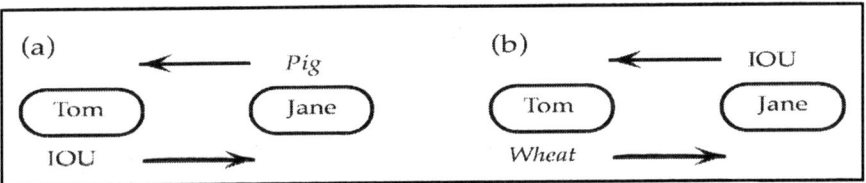

Figure 9.1 *A split barter. (a) Jane accepts Tom's promise (IOU) in exchange for one of her pigs. (b) When the wheat is ready, Tom exchanges some of his wheat for the IOU that Jane has held.*

story of specialisation as it is of technical innovation. Or to put it in Eric Beinhocker's terms, it is as much about *social innovation* as *technical innovation*[26].

Now suppose Tom would like a pig from Jane but Tom's wheat crop is not yet ready to harvest. If Jane trusts Tom she might be willing to give him the pig now and have Tom give her the wheat when it's ready. But suppose Tom is a stickler, and he writes a formal little note that says "Tom owes Jane one pig's worth of wheat" and gives it to Jane in exchange for the pig. Later, at harvest time, Tom delivers the wheat to Jane and she gives him the note in exchange, since she doesn't want to claim any more wheat from Tom. Tom can throw the note in the fire, because he has fulfilled his promise and the note has no more purpose.

It may be helpful to show this as a little diagram, as shown in Figure 9.1. Tom's note is depicted as IOU (I owe you: Tom's promise to Jane). There are two stages. In the first, they exchange Jane's pig for Tom's IOU. In the second, they exchange the IOU for Tom's wheat. For reasons we'll soon get to, it is helpful to describe the two-stage process as *split barter*, a term invented by an insightful but little-known thinker E. C. Riegel[70].

This kind of exchange is easy when there are only two people and two products, but what if there are three?

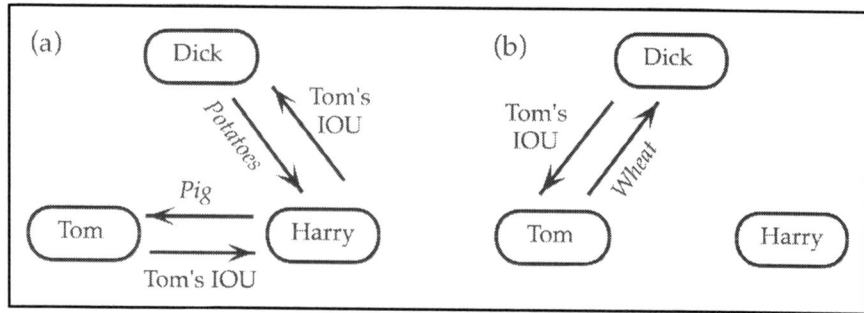

Figure 9.2 *A three-way split barter.*

The well-known problem with barter is that you have to find someone who has what you want, and who wants what you have. Suppose Harry has a pig, but he doesn't want Tom's wheat, he wants Dick's potatoes. Dick wants Tom's wheat (which is not ready yet), but Tom doesn't want Dick's potatoes, he wants Harry's pig.

Now it happens there's a three-way match here, and if they're patient and trusting they might do the three-way barter. Again Tom wants to write a note, an IOU, formalising his debt because his wheat is not ready. Then the exchanges can proceed as follows, and as depicted in Figure 9.2. Harry exchanges a pig for Tom's IOU. If Dick knows and trusts Tom, he might be willing to accept Tom's IOU from Harry in exchange for giving Harry some of his potatoes. (Tom might have phrased his note "Tom owes the bearer wheat to the value of one pig.") Later, when Tom's wheat is ready, Dick can present Tom's IOU and get some wheat in return. This is also a split barter, occurring in three stages.

In this example, Tom's IOU will have *circulated as money*. This will be more obvious if more people become involved in the exchanges. For example Dick might pass Tom's IOU to Mary in exchange for a coat, and Mary might pass it to Fred in exchange for fixing her roof. For this to work, Mary and Fred will also need to know Tom and trust his IOU, his promise. If finally Fred wants some wheat he can present it to Tom at harvest time and Tom's debt is extinguished. He can throw the note in the fire. That Tom's note has functioned as money will be more evident shortly, when I show the same functions being performed by a more familiar form of money.

First, however, we can begin to see the power of Tom's note, and the split barter it enables. Tom's note has facilitated a series of exchanges. Those exchanges would have been hard to arrange as direct barter. Tom's note enables a series of half-exchanges: goods and services from from person to person, but in any one exchange there is no good or service offered in return, only the note. Each person eventually does a second exchange, so everything balances out in the end. What could have required a lot of discussion and bargaining is accomplished with a minimum of fuss.

So Tom's note was a *medium of exchange* – a means of facilitating exchange. Because exchange is the fundamental economic act, this medium of exchange operates at a fundamental level, and it is powerful because it makes exchange so much easier. This form of money has some important properties, which we can now look at.

Tom's note is *token money*, money with no intrinsic value of its own: it is just a piece of paper with some words on it. The role of token money is to permit *split barter*, and the power of split barter is that people doing exchanges don't have to have matching wants. Tom can do half of an exchange with Harry, and later he can do the other half with Dick (or whoever bears his note).

It would have been possible to do an indirect exchange among Tom, Dick and Harry, using Harry's pig as an intermediary. In other words Dick could have exchanged some potatoes for Harry's pig, even though Dick didn't want a pig. Later Dick could exchange the pig for Tom's

163

wheat. In this case the pig would function as money, as the medium of exchange. Historically people have used pigs, tobacco, grain and other commodities in this way as media of exchange. We might call them *commodity money*, in contrast to Tom's note, which is token money. Commodity money has its own intrinsic value, whereas token money does not.

Tom's note represents a *debt*. With the introduction of debt comes *risk*. The risk arises because we can't be sure what the future will bring. If Tom's crop is destroyed by a hailstorm, Jane will lose – she gave a pig but got only a piece of paper in return. So token money introduces *debt and risk.*

Commodity money does not involve debt, because everyone has full value all the time and no promises or notes are necessary. However commodities are less convenient, and their value may change. The pig will need to be cared for, and it might die.

In the first example above, with Tom and Jane, we can see more clearly that Tom's note is really the expression of a *social contract* between Tom and Jane. Because it is a contract, it was created when the agreement was made and it can be destroyed when the agreement is fulfilled. (With this perspective, we don't have to be horrified that money is sometimes destroyed – Tom burnt his note, and a bank de-issues or destroys money as a loan is payed off).

When we recognise money as a contract, we can see two sides to it. To the giver of the note, it represents a *promise* to deliver a service – as has been explicit in our examples. On the other hand to the bearer of the note it represents a *claim* on someone else's service (in this case, Tom's). The ten dollar note in your wallet carries an implicit promise, and gives you a claim. The claim is on your community, for ten dollars' worth of goods or services. The implicit promise from your community is to supply you with those goods or services, just as Tom promised to supply wheat.

These examples allow us to be clear about what money is – what its function is and what properties it has. It's function is to facilitate exchange, to be a medium of exchange. The token money illustrated here represents an implicit contract, involving a promise and a claim. The promise is that at some point in the future goods or services will be supplied. The promise involves a *debt*. Because the future is uncertain, the promise involves *risk.*

This kind of money, token money, does not seem to be backed by anything. At some times in the past, paper money could (at least supposedly) be exchanged for gold. Gold would be a form of commodity money, and it has certainly had that function in many societies. There was no mention of gold in the above examples. Rather than saying token money is backed by nothing, I think it is more accurate to say it is backed by trust within the community. Tom's note would not have circulated if people did not trust Tom, and each other. Thus this kind of token money depends on the existence of a trusting community, as does the worth of any contract.

Here we encounter yet more contradictions in the neoliberal view. The neoclassical theory assumes competition and derides cooperation, so trust is implicitly derided, yet the money we commonly use is token money that requires trust for it to hold its value. The neoliberal ideology extols markets and derides centralised government control, yet the value of our money, the rules of its issue, and the interest that it draws all depend on central authorities.

Returning to the properties of token money, it *links the future to the present.* This is a bit technical, but it is critical to the role token money may play in the unfolding of an economy. Tom's note represents a claim on *future* service.

165

The contract between Tom and Jane therefore links the future to the present, because Jane must agree to hold her wish for some wheat in abeyance, expecting the agreement to be fulfilled in the future.

This linking of the future to the present is fundamentally important for understanding the dynamics of an economic system, as it means, in the language of calculus, the primary signalling mechanism in the system involves time-derivatives. The neoclassical theory deals with a static equilibrium that excludes time, so it excludes this crucial property of token money and cannot describe the way economies develop over time, nor properly describe the role and influence of money.

So far the discussion has been in terms of Tom's note, which still may not seem much like normal money. To make the connection clearer, suppose the people in Tom's community like the way his note helped them to exchange things, but they realise it would be more useful if they could use a standardised form of note, or promise. So (moving the story right along) they get the local printer to print up some notes that say "The bearer is owed goods or services to the value of one dollar", and they agree that one dollar stands for the value of one kilogram of wheat. They also ask the printer to keep track of how many notes are issued to each person who wants some, in other words to keep track of each person's promises. The printer decides to set up a side business to perform the note-printing and accounting, for which he will of course charge an appropriate fee. The printer decides to call this business Community Bank.

In this new arrangement, Tom can withdraw some notes from the Bank, which records a debit balance in Tom's account. Tom can then use the notes as he used his IOU, exchanging them for some goods. Harry and Dick can use the notes as they used Tom's IOU. When the notes return to

Tom, he can deposit them and eliminate his debit balance at the bank.

The standardised notes function in just the way Tom's note functioned, to facilitate exchange. They also have the same properties – they represent a contract, they are tokens backed by trust within the community, they represent debt and therefore carry risk, and they link the future to the present.

Although I have stressed so far that token money can operate in a trusting community, not all exchange occurs in such a context of trust. There are societies in which neither central authority nor social custom are strong, and there is little trust in international dealings. In situations where trust is lacking it *does* make sense for money to be backed by things of real value. Bernard Lietaer[71] has therefore proposed a *backed currency*, which he calls a *Terra*, backed by a 'basket' of commodities that can be stored in warehouses. It could be beneficial especially for poorer countries whose currencies may be vulnerable to global forces. The particular mix of commodities would be determined by each country using those of its products that best retain their value.

There are passionate advocates of backing money with gold, as money used to be (or was alleged to be) before the "gold standard" was discarded. However gold is neither necessary nor very good as a backing commodity. Token money, in a trusting community, does not need to be backed by gold or any other commodity. It's true that in order to maintain a steady value the money supply must be carefully managed, but that is a different issue. Anyway the value of gold is also volatile, depending as it does on arbitrary fluctuations in supply as gold discoveries are made, on hoarding, and on peoples' highly subjective valuation of gold as an ornament, as an imperishable commodity or even as a symbol of immortality. Gold may *seem* real and substantial, and it is, but its *value* is almost as arbitrary as the value of a fancy piece of paper with a number on it.

How should we finance investment?

Suppose Mary, in our little community with the Community Bank, wants to open a shop to sell the clothing she and her friends make. She needs money to renovate a building and set up her business. How can she raise the money she needs?

One way would be to withdraw as many notes as she needs from the Community Bank and spend them with tradesmen and suppliers. She would then have a large debit balance at the Bank. Another way to say it is that she would have made a lot of promises around the town: she would have received a lot of goods and services and would only have given pieces of paper in return. In other words she would have a large debt. However you put it, she needs to earn enough money to pay back the money she withdrew, to reduce her debit balance, to fulfil her implicit promises so supply goods or services to the community.

There are two problems with funding Mary's shop in this way. One is that the amount of money circulating in the community would have suddenly risen. This might have caused prices of other things to rise. As she paid back her debts, the amount of money would decrease. If people had got used to the extra money circulating, they might have adjusted to a higher level of exchanges. If then the amount of money shrank, prices might fall, business slow and some people have to adjust to slower business. In other words the issue of a large amount of money as a loan to Mary could cause a mini-boom, and mini-bust. There is a better way, which we'll get to.

The other problem is that if Mary's business does not thrive she may have to abandon the idea of running the shop. She might then be unable to pay her debts. She would be unable to fulfil the promises she had made. The money she spent would then lose value, because people would be unable to claim the value implicitly promised to them.

This option, to create new money to fund Mary's new shop, thus leads to the same problems we have seen in our larger society. Because bank loans are made up mostly of new money created out of nothing, the supply of money is entangled with the investment process. The supply of money is prone to fluctuate with investment activity, and an investment failure can rebound on the value of money.

Perhaps Mary should save money until she has enough to start her shop. This seems like a more responsible thing to do, but there are still a couple of catches, depending on how she goes about it. If she simply stashes notes under her mattress until she has enough, she is accumulating promises and depriving people of the opportunity to discharge their debts, until such time as she is ready to spend the money. It means, in effect, her community has to hold in abeyance the capacity to repay the claims on goods and services she has accumulated. Also the supply of circulating money will fall while some of it is stuck under Mary's mattress.

These may not seem like serious problems, but there are real-world equivalents of these too. China has accumulated a large trade surplus with the United States. This means China has significant power over the US economy. This power is magnified because China refuses to allow its currency, the yuan, to increase in value relative to the US dollar, because that keeps Chinese exports relatively cheap. This puts the US at a disadvantage, because it makes US exports more expensive. These problems are not as widely recognised, outside trade policy circles, as domestic economic issues, but they are a threat nevertheless. The underlying problem is still that too much debt is accumulated, and debt is destabilising.

Instead of simply putting her money under the mattress, Mary might deposit it back with the Community Bank. The Bank could then credit her account and re-issue the notes to other people. However Mary would still be accumulating promises, and the same underlying problems would be there. There would still be debts left outstanding.

It may seem these problems are just intrinsic to using money. Money involves promises, debts and risks, but it is so useful we just have to put up with the problems. To a degree this is true, but what if we can minimise the problems and maximise the benefit? Our present system, we'll come to see, magnifies the problems and reduces the benefit. However money, finance and investment can be organised in other ways. Though this is not widely appreciated, the essence of how to do things better has been known for over a century. For example, one of the most insightful thinkers on alternative ways to organise money and investment was Silvio Gessell, writing around the turn of the last century[72].

Before getting to alternatives, it's instructive to look at a historical example (the discussion of Mary's options for investing may seem a bit too hypothetical, though they are based in historical events). During the Great Depression, there was plenty of work that needed to be done, and plenty of people capable of doing it, as is true in any depression. What was lacking was money, a medium of exchange, a way of organising and enabling people to do what needed to be done. Quite a few people understood this, and there were many attempts to organise some kind of local exchange system that would replace the failed national currency systems. Many of these were not well designed, and they did not survive. However a couple of these experiments did work, in Austria and Germany. Their stories are very instructive.

Pre-empting Hitler – the path not taken

In 1932 the town of Wörgl in Austria was severely depressed. Unemployment was about 30% and the town was having difficulty paying its workers because citizens had fallen behind in paying their taxes. About 200 families were penniless. Conditions were as bad in neighbouring towns as well. There were many things that needed to be done in the town, such as re-paving the streets, and extending the town's water supply. There were also people able to do the work. The problem was a lack of money, which was caused by the economic depression.

Rather than spending the meagre 40,000 schillings on hand directly on town works, Mayor Michael Unterguggenberger decided to bank it as a guarantee to back the issue by the town of a kind of money called stamp scrip. For this scrip to remain valid, a stamp to the value of 1% of the scrip's face value had to be pasted on the back every month. In effect, the value of the money declined by 1% per month. The money was issued by paying the town employees half in official money and half in stamp scrip money.

Since no-one wanted to be holding the money at the end of the month, they spent it as fast as they could. This was really not a problem, since people were desperate anyway for the things they could buy with it. Some even paid their taxes early. Stores agreed to accept the scrip because people did not have much official money anyway, and because they would lose business to rival stores if they did not accept it. In this way the stamp scrip spread through the entire community and was used for many things besides public works.

For a period of about a year, activity in the town increased substantially, unemployment fell by 25%, and the town was able to undertake long-neglected public works. The fees collected from the stamp scrip were used to feed over 200 destitute families. Investment in productive assets in Wörgl jumped by over 200% within a year. The town began to prosper in the midst of severe depression. Neighbouring villages copied the idea because it was working so well, and within a year mayors from all over Austria were wanting to know about "the miracle of Wörgl".

The idea of stamp scrip had been developed by Silvio Gessell, who published his penetrating ideas late in the nineteenth century[73]. The stamp scrip money in Wörgl circulated at about 12 times the rate of official money, because people always spent the stamp scrip first, so as to minimise the cost of the stamps required to keep it current. As a result the money issued by the town was far more effective at stimulating (or rather, facilitating) local economic activity than if the Mayor had just spent his meagre supply of official currency on public works.

Similar events had unfolded at Schwanenkirchen in Germany, a small village in which the main industry was a coal mine. The mine was in danger of closing, but the owner offered to keep it open if his workers would agree to be paid 90% of their wages in stamp scrip. This scrip was backed by the value of the coal they would extract from the mine. The workers did agree, and within a few months the town had returned to prosperity in the midst of Germany's depression. This scrip circulated widely outside Schwanenkirchen and became the focus of a Free Economy (Freiwirtschaft) movement in Germany. Over 2000 corporations throughout Germany started to use the alternative currency.

Schwanenkirchen and Wörgl attracted considerable attention, and many other Austrian and German towns showed interest in issuing stamp scrip. However in the cases of both Schwanenkirchen (1931) and Wörgl (1933) the national governments intervened and outlawed the scrip. They did this under pressure from their central banks, whose monopoly was threatened. Wörgl sued the Austrian central bank, and the case went to the Austrian Supreme Court, but was lost. So the towns returned to high unemployment, despair and desperation.

The fortunes of the Nazi Party in Germany generally followed the level of unemployment[71]. Between 1924 and 1928, following the disastrous period of hyper-inflation of Germany's official currency, unemployment declined from 340,000 to 268,000 and the Nazi share of seats gained in elections declined from 6.6% to 2.6%. By September 1930 unemployment had risen to over 1 million and the Nazis held 18% of seats. By March 1933, unemployment was 5.6 million and the Nazis held 44% of seats. In November 1933 they gained 92% of seats.

Many unofficial exchange or currency experiments were also tried in the United States during the 1930s depression, although they were not always well set up and some of

173

them did not succeed[73]. The eminent economist Irving Fisher, together with Hans Cohrssen, proposed in 1933 that stamp scrip be introduced officially into the US[74], but their proposal was turned down on the grounds that it would undermine the established monetary system[75].

Instead President Roosevelt borrowed official currency to fund the work-creation projects of the New Deal. Although these projects helped many people, their effects were marginal and the United States did not really emerge from the depression until it became involved in World War II.

The German path out of depression was through Fascism, which quickly led to war. The United States only emerged from depression when the requirements of war forced it to re-organise its production systems. Part of that re-organisation involved the issuing of a great deal more money than had been available during the 1930s.

Schwanenkirchen and Wörgl also emerged from depression, although only briefly. They followed a quite different path, a path that involved local initiative, free enterprise and a well-designed currency that liberated the local initiative and enterprise. These towns required no help from their national governments. All they required was to be left to prosper.

There is a larger lesson here. The depression was caused by a failure of organisation, not by a lack of resources, talent or initiative. In each example, depression was overcome by a change of organisation. The crucial change is most readily apparent from the cases of Wörgl and Schwanenkirchen – the crucial change is to ensure a sufficient supply of currency, which allows people to do what they want to do.

Keeping the money flowing

Stamp scrip money is peculiarly different from the money we are used to. If we save conventional money and deposit it in a bank, the bank will pay us. The payment is called *interest*, and is paid as a percentage of our total balance. If we saved stamp scrip we would instead have to pay, because the money requires a new stamp every month. In effect, there is a percentage fee due on the money, instead of a percentage payment accruing from the money.

Stamp scrip money will seem strange and unworkable upon first encounter. In effect its value declines with time, so after a while it would be worth little or nothing. What good is money whose value shrinks away? How would anyone ever save for the future? There are good answers to those questions. The answers are that stamp scrip money is good for facilitating exchange, and you can save by other means. To understand how, we need to explore further.

The Wörgl economy prospered because the stamp scrip facilitated many more exchanges than the official national money. Even though there was no more of it paid out by the Mayor, it circulated faster, and thus accomplished more. To be clear, it would not cause anyone to work more than they wanted, it merely allowed them to do what they already wanted.

A central problem in a depression is that money is hoarded and does not circulate as fast as it would in normal times. Even if banks have plenty of money available, they are cautious about lending it out when times are bad. People are reluctant to borrow for the same reason, and if they are unemployed they can't borrow anyway. On top of that, prices fall as a depression takes hold (deflation, the opposite of inflation). Prices fall because there is less money available.

If prices are falling, it makes sense to hold onto your money if you can, because things will be cheaper later. This only exacerbates the shortage of money and makes prices fall further. The invisible foot stomps with a vengeance.

With their talent for obscuring simple ideas with strange jargon, economists call this phenomenon a *liquidity trap*. Liquidity means spendable money. Instead of circulating, money falls into "holes", like bank vaults and people's savings accounts, and gets trapped there.

Because nobody wants to hold on to shrinking money, it doesn't get caught in the "liquidity traps". It will circulated as fast as people want it to, in other words it will facilitate as many exchanges as people are willing and able to do. People can get on with their routine affairs, with business as usual. In a depression, the amount of conventional money decreases, and what is left circulates more slowly, so business as usual is impeded.

In Chapter 2 I raised the question of why a failure of some investments should interfere with other people's business as usual. Why does a failure on Wall Street bring down Main Street? The answer, I indicated there, is that the supply of money goes up and down with the financial markets. This in turn is because money is supplied in the course of banks making "loans". It seems shrinking money might avoid this problem, because money can be supplied independently of the financial markets, and because it will keep circulating even if business slows. However this raises the issue of how investment can work in conjunction with a system of shrinking money.

Saving money or saving wealth?

We are used to thinking of saving in terms of money: you save some money and deposit it in a bank. The banks pays you a small amount of interest. Later you can withdraw your money. However the bank has not just held your money while you are not using it. The bank instead has invested some of your money (let's keep this from being too complicated, by assuming this is a good, old-fashioned, well-behaved savings bank that does indeed invest your money, rather than playing speculative games with it in the financial markets). The bank retains a fraction of its depositors' money to cover those who will want to withdraw some, but loans the rest out. The returns on those loan investments are the reason the bank can afford to pay you a modest rate of interest on your deposit.

However the money we use is not itself wealth, it is only a token of wealth. Your money doesn't sit in the bank vault after you deposit it in your savings account. Rather, the bank issues it back into circulation, in the course of investing it through a new loan, let's say to build a factory. In the meantime you are credited with the value you have deposited. So what has really happened is that your money has enabled another kind of exchange. The value you have accumulated, which is *represented (betokened)* by some token money, has been *exchanged* for a share of a factory. The *money* you used as a token of your saved value is thereby released to facilitate other exchanges.

If the money you deposit doesn't really sit in the bank in the form of token money, then it doesn't matter what form of token money you use. You could as well use shrinking money. In that case, you could specify to the bank that you want the value converted into (exchanged for) something of real present value, like a share in a factory. In this way the wealth that you deposit will not sit there shrinking away to nothing, its value will be retained, or even increase. More simply, you could open a savings account and deposit it there, instead of in the "demand" account that you use for your daily business – what is commonly called a checking account.

In other words your bank can offer two services. One service is to supply currency for your daily business. The other service is a savings and investment scheme, whereby the bank undertakes to invest your money in things that will retain or increase their value. The latter is what old-fashioned savings banks used to do (also variously known as credit unions or savings and loans), and normally retail banks still offer these services.

This means that *savings* can operate in the normal way in the presence of a shrinking money system. There is in fact no problem at all combining savings with a shrinking money system, once we get clear that it's not the actual money (the tokens of value) that are saved.

However there is still a big potential question regarding *investment.* In many people's minds, investment is done with savings. In the capitalist myth, investment is done with the capitalist's savings (never mind how much he has screwed everyone else to accumulate his savings). However in the real modern world a great deal of "investment" is done with money created out of nothing.

The example of Mary wanting to open a new shop shows that this issue exists even in the simplest, community-scale monetary system. Creating new money for investments links the supply of money to the investment process. This is what exposes the whole economy to the vagaries of investment (not to mention speculation). The supply of currency people need for their business as usual goes up and down as investment goes up and down, and the whole economy is exposed to the risks that are inevitably involved with investment. If speculation plays a large role in the financial system, then the risks are much greater. Everyone is exposed to the follies of the big-money casino that our financial markets have become.

Separating the money supply from investment

We have distinguished two processes, providing a medium of exchange, and mediating savings and loans. I have argued the provision of currency needs to be kept separate from the provision of loans for investment. We can flesh out some more detail about how these processes can be implemented, starting with the provision of currency.

The money supplied by the Community Bank in the earlier example can be obtained routinely. The process operates like a line of credit or a credit card, though the fees will be charged differently. Money is a medium of exchange and exchange is the fundamental economic action, so it makes complete sense to be able to get and use money as and when we need to exchange. There do need to be some limits, which we'll get to shortly. In this way the supply of money can be separated from investing.

It is such a habit to think of money as valuable, it may seem strange to be able to obtain money at will, within limits, but the process is no more mysterious than using a credit card. The bank keeps track of how much you have withdrawn. That amount represents the implicit promises you have made, to sell goods or services (including "serving" your employer) to earn the money to pay back to your account.

Now let's look at how to set up a system of "shrinking" money, money that comes with an incentive not to hoard but to spend, so it will keep circulating, doing its good work.

There have been many small-scale trials of such "alternative currencies", and people have learnt what works reasonably well[71,76]. The best kind seems to be what is called a Mutual Credit Union (mutual because, in effect, we grant credit to each other).

There are three main considerations. There need to be limits on how much customers can withdraw. The MCU needs to have an income to support the operation. Customers should be discouraged from either withdrawing too much or from hoarding. These goals can be met if there are limits and percentage fees on *both* debit and credit balances. The fee on a debit balance is analogous to the fee on a credit card balance, although here interpreted as a charge for the privilege of being supplied with a medium of exchange. The fee on a credit balance is like the stamp on stamp scrip. It discourages customers from using an MCU account as a place to save. Saving is to be done elsewhere, as we'll get to.

If you have a credit balance, it's better to spend any extra cash in hand back into circulation. If you have a debit balance, it's better to deposit your cash to reduce your debit balance and the fees accumulating on it. This fee structure works to limit the number of promises you make (by withdrawing and spending money) and the number of claims you hold (by holding on to money). The fees would be supplemented by limits on the total debit or credit balance you are allowed. The debit limit would be like the limit on your credit card balance. The credit limit would mean you have to spend cash in hand rather than depositing it. Really there would be little reason to maintain a credit balance anyway.

(Just as an aside, the terms *credit* and *debit* are often confusing, because we commonly don't say explicitly *whose* credit or *whose* debit. If you charge something to your credit card, the bank is granting you credit, and you are acquiring a debit balance. For every credit there is a corresponding debit. In just the same way, if you withdraw money from the *Credit* Union you acquire a *debit* balance.)

The MCU needs an income to support its operation, and the fees provide that source. The magnitude of the fees is something that would be best decided in practice. Relatively large percentage fees seem to be recommended, like the stamp scrip fee of 1% per month. This may seem exorbitant, but everyone is encouraged to keep their balances small, so customers need not pay a lot. In the same way you can avoid large fees on your credit card by paying it off promptly when due.

The business of the MCU needs to be seen strictly as the provision of a medium of exchange. The fees pay for this service. As this service plays a strategic role in the economy, and there is a clear potential for abuse (witness our present banking system), there is a clear case for it being regulated to minimise abuse. It could reasonably be regarded in the same way as the court system – a service of strategic importance to society, and therefore one to be closely overseen. Thus it would not be like any other private enterprise, it would be a public service. There is thus a strong case for MCUs to be non-profit organisations.

Turning now to a savings and loan (S&L) system, this does not require much further explanation. The S&Ls role would be to take deposits and convert them into suitable investments, and to convert them back into money when a customer desired. It could be run in conjunction with an MCU, for the convenience of customers, though the two businesses would need to be clearly separated.

Decentralised or centralised?
Government debts, inflation

So far this discussion of money and investment has been presented in terms of a small community, but that was only to keep the ideas clear. There is no reason the same systems could not be run at larger scales. Larger firms would have bigger turnovers and potentially desire more investment finance, so larger financial institutions would be required to service them – within reason. The United States traditionally had many local and regional banks, as well as a few at the national scale. The giant banks now dominate, but the viability of a multilayered system is not in doubt. MCUs and S&Ls could also operate at several scales.

There is a question as to whether money could be supplied in a decentralised way, with many local and regional MCUs, or whether it should operate in a centralised way. In most countries at present the monetary system is highly centralised. Reserve banks are in charge of regulating the issue of money, including the setting of interest rates. However there is no reason in principle why local money systems could not operate. There are advantages and disadvantages either way.

In the pre-Civil-War US, the issuing of money was almost totally unregulated, and almost anyone could set themselves up as money-issuing banks. Exchanging among the many currencies became a business in itself. This time saw the origin of the expression "Show me the colour of your money". Typically currencies from more distant sources would be accepted only at a large discount, or not at all. Counterfeiters flourished.[77] So the absence of any regulation clearly brings problems.

At the other extreme, money issue these days is mostly centrally controlled by national authorities, usually central banks that may or may not be under the authority of government; the US Federal Reserve is an uneasy semi-private alliance between banks and the national government. This gives uniformity, but the involvement of private banks exacts a heavy cost on the economy in the form of interest. It also leaves the system vulnerable to manipulation for the advantage of private banks, a major problem in the US.

There is another curious consequence of this kind of centralised system. Because the supply of currency is, at least nominally, under the authority of the national government, and because currency is issued through loans that are spent into circulation by the government, national governments incur large debts that some regard as a threat to government solvency. In combination with neoliberals' aversion to anything to do with governments, this has led to an obsession with balancing the government budget, as though the money-issuing authority is like a household or a business. This is quite misguided.

The issue can be clarified by referring back to our MCU. If a client wants to spend some money they can withdraw some from their account at the MCU. This leaves them with a debt to the MCU, until such time as they might earn money and pay off that debt. However if everyone were to reduce their debt to zero, there would be no money in circulation. The whole point is to incur the debt that is intrinsic to money (the IOU) so we can have a convenient medium of exchange.

Now if we say the MCU is like the Reserve Bank, and if its one customer were the government, then if the government were truly to pay off its entire debt there would be no money left in circulation. It's not really that simple or dire, because the rest of us can still get money from the banks, but the money spent into circulation by the government is a considerable fraction of all the money, so if the government, in effect, pulls money out of circulation the economy will slow. This might be sensible if there is excessive debt and money in circulation, as in a boom. However it is not sensible if the economy is depressed.

One current manifestation of this misconception is that "austerity" policies intended to reduce government deficits reduce the amount of money in circulation and thus stifle the economy. The European Central Bank is currently the most ardent practitioner of austerity, and its imposition of austerity on Europe's struggling peripheral countries has worsened their depression. So even central bankers don't understand the system they are running.

The obsessions with austerity and balancing the budgets of national governments are misguided in those countries in which the government controls the issue of currency. The government will never go broke, because it can always create more money to pay its debts. Governments that control such *sovereign currencies* are not like households or businesses that must eventually earn the money to pay off their debts. Unfortunately for the peripheral countries of Europe, they have ceded their money-creating power to the European Central Bank, by agreeing to use the Euro currency, so it is possible for them to go broke. That only makes the ECB's austerity policy more foolish, because it makes it even harder for the struggling countries to pay their debts.

The great fear of the deficit hawks is that issuing money will cause ruinous inflation. Inflation occurs when there is too much money chasing too few goods and services. That is not a problem during a recession, because during a recession there is not enough money to keep the economy functioning at full capacity. Any extra money will be soaked up by bringing unused capacity back into use. On the other hand when the economy is operating near full capacity (full employment and factories operating at full capacity), production cannot be easily increased as the money supply increases, so that is when inflation is a threat.

In our present system there are major incentives for the private banks to increase the money supply, and central authorities have left themselves with only very weak means of controlling the money supply. In an MCU system the incentives for customers are to minimise the amount of money in circulation, and MCUs could be prohibited from arbitrarily increasing limits on balances. Thus an MCU and a complementary savings and loan system would not be nearly as prone to abuse, so inflation ought to be much less of a threat. If it did threaten, authorities could manage the money supply rather more directly through restrictions on balance limits and on the fees charged. A centralised system operating on the same principles as an MCU would allow the money supply to be managed even more directly.

There is a school of thought called Modern Money Theory[78] that argues that the current system of centrally-issued token money can be used to eliminate unemployment, and that government deficits are never a problem because the government can always cause more money to be issued.[79]

Even in the relatively healthy economies of the recent past, real unemployment rates have been more like 10% or more (official statistics seriously and deliberately understate unemployment and ignore under-employment), and much higher in the present depressed economies. So economies have been operating well below capacity. Inflation has been an issue because of the dysfunctional money system

185

in which debt can be too readily created, not because it is inevitable in a well-designed system.

Save from our own efforts, don't borrow from our children

If Main Street is to be insulated from the vagaries of Wall Street, then currency needs to be supplied independently from making loans. Not only does there need to be an independent source of money, like the Mutual Credit Union just described, but new money should not be issued as part of a loan. This means that loans should *only* be made from savings. This is a big departure from long-established practice. It would require a careful transition from our current debt-based system to a savings-based system, but in terms of a business's costs there need not be a great difference between the present borrow-and-repay system *versus* a save-and-invest system. In fact businesses could still borrow, but they would be borrowing savings rather than, implicitly, from the future. There would be a big benefit, for businesses and for everyone, because they would be operating in a much more stable economy.

For bankers this change would mean the end of the fractional reserve system, but for everyone else it would mean there would be far less debt hanging over the economy and generating instability. It would also mean the end of what amounts to a private tax on money, which means a private tax on the entire economy.

Because bank "loans" are made up mostly of new money, interest is charged on the money that is issued. Although superficially this interest charge may seem to be not much different from the fee charge by an MCU on a debit account, there are key functional differences.

186

One difference is that the MCU plus savings bank system is designed to minimise debt. It does this by preventing the MCU from promoting the issue of new money, and by encouraging the rapid circulation of such money as is issued. On the other hand banks' incentive is to push loans on to people, and the money issued in the process does not circulate as rapidly, so more is required. Thus the present system generates more debt, especially if a speculative property bubble inflates.

It follows that the cost of money in the MCU system is less than it is in the present system, probably much less. The MCU fee charged is for the service of providing a medium of exchange, and it needs to be regarded as a public service not a function to be exploited for maximum profit. On the other hand the present system generates much more debt and thus involves a much greater cost to users, because of the interest charged. Thus the burden of interest payments due on issued money is overall much larger than it needs to be, and would be in an MCU system.

Interest-burdened money – the hidden private tax

At present money is borrowed into existence with a burden of interest due on it for a long as it circulates. Because the amounts of money and debt increase over the long term, this imposes a long-term cost on the economy. The cost is surprisingly large. One example of this will be familiar to home buyers. Over the twenty-year term of a typical mortgage, the amount of interest paid can be more than the principal of the loan, sometimes as much as twice the principal.

Because most people borrow more than they lend, they pay more interest than they receive. Only the rich lend more than they borrow. The result is a large transfer of wealth to the already wealthy. One estimate of this transfer is shown in Figure 9.3, which shows the net flows of interest to or from different income categories for one year in Germany. This flow of interest is not just from mortgages, it is from all borrowings, which are necessary to maintain the money supply.

The supply of money to the economy is of course a service, and the service needs to be paid for one way or another. Abraham Lincoln supplied money directly to the economy during the civil war by printing "greenbacks" and

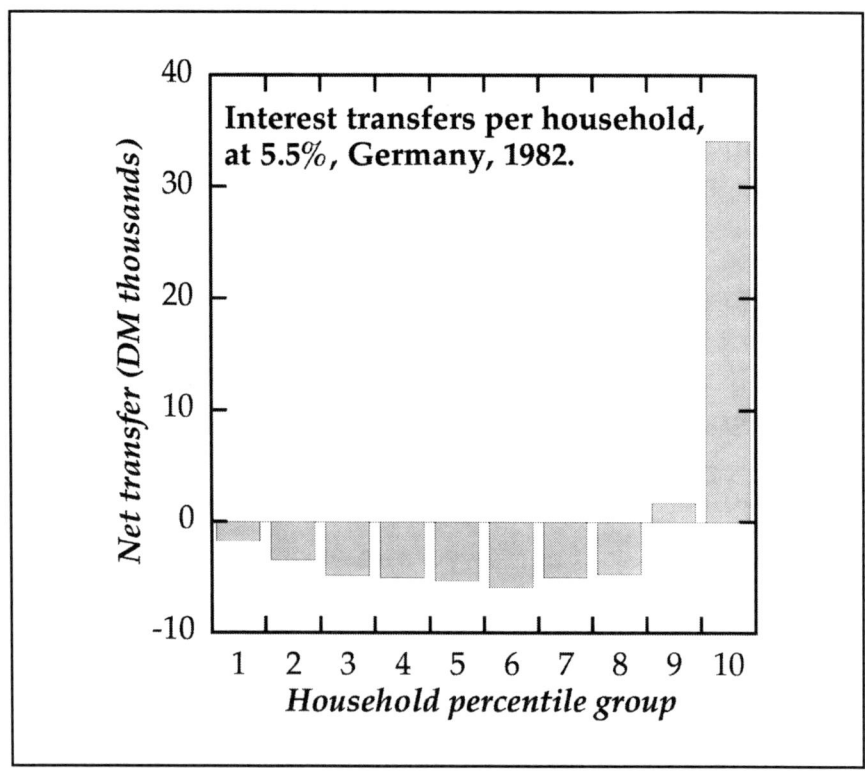

Figure 9.3. Net transfers among income groups, in thousands of Deutschmark per household[75]. Household incomes are grouped by every ten percentiles, i.e. by decile. Even in 1982 households in the middle income range paid around 5,000 DM net in interest, whereas households in the top decile received about 34,000 DM.

using them to buy services for the government[80]. Lincoln considered it the government's role to provide a stable currency for the citizenry. No fee or interest was charged on the money. The cost was therefore borne ultimately by the whole economy, but it would have been minimal.

In the MCU system there is an explicit fee, but the cost will be much smaller than the costs shown in Figure 9.3 because the system minimises debt. Because the cost is identified explicitly as a fee for service, it will be subject to adjustment by market forces. It would be possible, for example, for another bank to compete by charging less.

In contrast, the amount of interest charged on money in our present system is subject to adjustment by central authorities for extraneous purpose of regulating the money supply, or at least attempting to. There is also a more fundamental problem with charging interest. This problem relates not just to supplying a medium of exchange, it is a general problem applying to any kind of loan.

Interest – a market failure

Charging interest brings about a market failure, which is why it has been morally proscribed by many societies. The problem is that if you charge interest you make a profit without having to share any of the risk in generating that profit. The risk is entirely born by the borrower. It is a fundamental requirement in a market system that relevant risks be factored into any investment. Capital will only be allocated efficiently if both earning capacity and risk are properly assessed in investment decisions. It was the disconnection of subprime lenders from the risks of the investment that allowed the US subprime mortgage bubble to grow so large before it collapsed.

The borrower, on the other hand, is required to bear all of the risk. Borrowers are bound to an inflexible requirement that takes no account either of the risks of investment or of the vagaries of life. The arrangement is unbalanced.

Charging interest is proscribed by Islam, and in some circumstances by Judaism. It used to be proscribed in Christianity as well. Islam does not proscribe gaining income from an investment, it proscribes fixed interest as the means of gaining that income. A fairer way of gaining income from an investment is by replacing interest with a share of profits – or losses – as is the case if you buy shares in a company.

The unfairness inherent in charging interest often might not be very apparent but it is there, perhaps more obviously in poor countries. According to Mohammad Yunus[81], extreme poverty in Bangladesh almost invariably comes about through a poor family being forced into debt by a misfortune like illness. Commonly, because they are poor, their only recourse is to a loan shark who charges an exorbitant interest rate. It is often difficult for them to make repayments, and if they fail they may lose their land and livelihood to the lender. They may then become debt slaves, working for the lender to pay an unpayable debt.

In developed countries we have some protection through bankruptcy procedures. Unfortunately protections are few and loan sharks are plentiful in many poor societies. The same is true in the international environment: many poor countries are effectively in debt slavery to wealthy Western lenders.

There is thus a case for ultimately abolishing the charging of interest and replacing it with investment dividends The existing process of investment already offers the appropriate alternative structure, wherein investors share profits, risks and losses. However the present financial system is so unstable it is not appropriate for it to replace the payment of interest. The options described elsewhere in this book could go far to stabilising the financial system, the monetary system and the whole economy. As that comes to pass, the replacement of interest payments with returns on investments would become more feasible.

Multiple benefits

The two functions explored in this chapter are sufficient for a modern economy to proceed. Money can be supplied for routine business through institutions modelled after Mutual Credit Unions. Investment can be facilitated by saving and loan facilities. These institutions would bring about several major improvements on our present arrangements.

First, the supply of money would be separated from the investment process. This would go far towards insulating Main Street from Wall Street. The failure of someone's investment need not affect the availability of the medium of exchange. Thus the devastation of depressions would be avoided, and much of the steam would be taken out of the business "cycle", in which ups and downs of investment and speculation drag the whole economy up and down with them.

Second, the amount of debt in the economy would be dramatically reduced. Rather than creating new money for "investment" and paying back, people would save and invest. Even the amount of money required for routine business would be reduced, because shrinking money circulates faster. The reduction in debt would stabilise the whole economy.

Third, by funding investment from savings rather than by creating new money, we would be bearing the burden of investment ourselves and giving our children the gift of an improved economy. At present we pass to our children the burden of paying for our own indulgences, and on top of that we risk passing an economy made anaemic by dysfunctional systems.

Fourth, several of the main ways in which wealth is disproportionately channelled to the already wealthy would be eliminated or greatly limited.

The proposed reforms would thus remove one of the main destabilisers of economies, as well as ensuring that flows of wealth are more in proportion to contributions. The opportunities for some to avoid responsibility for the effects of extortionate and occasionally disastrous practices would also be greatly diminished.

This discussion has outlined alternative monetary and investment arrangements, and indicated their main effects without going into a lot of detail. The point here is to highlight the dysfunctions of the present system and to show that alternatives are possible. Many practicalities would of course still need to be worked out.

10

THEIR OWN PETARDS

NEOLIBERALS have a ready array of accusations and derogatory phrases to throw at anyone who questions their ways. Progressive taxation and social welfare arc *wealth transfer* programs. Progressives indulge in *social engineering.* Anyone who questions the existence or behaviour of the super-wealthy is engaging in *class warfare.* Anyone who advocates any kind of ethical consistency or tolerance is accused of trying to impose *political correctness.*

A petard, as it turns out, is not a rope you are hoisted with, it was a small bomb designed to blow holes in gates, but prone to misfire and injure the firer. Let's see in which direction these expressions emit their strongest blast. Mainstream economics provides the supposed justifications for neoliberal policies, so again mainstream economists are called to account.

Wealth transfers

We have, in this book, identified a number of mechanisms that pump wealth from the poor and middle class to the rich.

Financial market speculation

The financial markets are dominated by speculation and other activities whose sole objective is to siphon wealth from the productive economy. The amount of wealth involved is very large. Some indication might be obtained from the fact that financial sectors in the US and Australia now account for 30-40% of corporate profits. Because corporate profits would be a large fraction of GDP, this means a significant fraction of total wealth is pumped to the rich by this mechanism.

Capturing emergent community wealth

This is the wealth that results from the proximity of individual assets and investments. It belongs to no individual, it belongs to the community. In some places some of this wealth is captured for community use, but very commonly the wealth passes as a windfall to private interests, much of it to developers and landlords. In this way small property holders and renters lose their share of community wealth to those rich enough to be able to capture it.

Interest charged on new money

Our money is created in the course of making loans, and interest is charged as though it were savings, rather than having been created out of nothing. Because we need money for the economy to function, this burden of interest weighs on the whole economy. Banks profit by maximising loans, so the amount of money in circulation is maximised, and this increases the burden on everyone. This is effectively a private tax on the entire economy, and we saw in Chapter 9 that it pumps wealth to the richest ten percent.

Access to loans

The rich can obtain loans much more easily than the poor. They can invest their loans and become even richer. This mechanism is widely recognised and clearly an important factor, though it is hard to estimate the amounts of wealth involved. Mohammed Yunus demonstrated, with his Grameen Bank in Bangladesh, that it is possible to give loans to the poorest people and so to reduce this iniquity[81].

The ownership escalator

We use only a restricted range of ownership options in our present economic system. As a result ownership is highly concentrated. Even though public corporations are owned collectively, it is the rich who own shares disproportionately. Even though many people own some shares through retirement funds, the distribution of ownership is still strongly skewed to the rich. Once you gain ownership of significant assets, wealth begins to flow to you. If you are poor and have to rent your accommodation, wealth drains away from you. Owners are on an up escalator. The poor are on a down escalator.

As William Greider observed, the problem is not that capital is privately owned, the problem is that most people don't own any. We already have many forms of ownership that can change this. Ownership can be distributed much more equitably by actively promoting less common forms such as ownership by employees and other stakeholders. Ownership can also be conditional, with time limits and

195

progressive transfers of ownership, or owning buildings but not land, and so on, as discussed in Chapter 7.

Corporate welfare

There are many subsidies paid to corporations or rich minorities that benefit the rich at the expense of the poor. Often they harm the environment as well, thus harming everyone. Even a decade ago perverse subsidies amounted to perhaps $2 trillion annually[82], a considerable fraction of global wealth generation.

Tax avoidance

This is closely related to corporate welfare, because it is practised mainly by large corporations, particularly transnational corporations. They do this by complex internal transfers of money that exploit loopholes in tax laws, or differences in tax systems among nations. They are abetted by a few small nations that charge minimal corporate tax. Such tax havens could be closed down overnight by concerted action of a few rich nations, but those nations' governments are owned by the rich, so it doesn't happen. The proportion of taxes collected from corporations has dropped by about half over the past half century.

This list will not be exhaustive, but it already demonstrates that vast amounts of wealth are transferred to the rich by mechanisms that cannot be justified as the fair operation of markets. Either the markets operate perversely, through the invisible fist instead of the invisible hand, or they have been rigged, with the connivance of compliant legislators. Corporate welfare and much tax avoidance result from explicit interventions. The other mechanisms are due to malfunctioning markets that allow some individuals to exploit an instability, an up escalator, that allows the rich to become richer.

Neoclassical economists, so unused to thinking about anything but equilibrium, are not good at recognising instabilities. A common example is that economies of scale allow the largest firms to grow until they dominate their market sector, as was discussed in Chapter 3. Many of the mechanisms listed above generate analogous instabilities, such that the more you have the more you are able to get, by fair means or foul.

Capturing emergent community wealth and interest charged on new money may be less well known mechanisms, but they were each identified a century or more ago. The authors of those insights (Henry George, Silvio Gessell, E. C. Riegel and others) have been ignored, ridiculed or both.

If we simply eliminated the mechanisms that unfairly pump wealth to the rich, our societies would be considerably less unequal. The need for welfare would be greatly reduced. The efficiency of the economy would be increased, because producers would pay closer to the full costs of production and costly welfare bureaucracies could be reduced. The dignity and self respect of the less wealthy would not be compromised by having to accept welfare, and by being perpetually robbed and vilified by the greedy. Fixing the problems at their sources would be far more efficient and effective than the various retroactive mechanisms that have been developed through the twentieth century.

By all means let us talk about wealth transfers, but let's look at it without ideological blinkers. Most of our economic activities are collaborative, and so require cooperation among various parties. We are a social species, and it is healthy and necessary for us to cede some of our autonomy in return for the greater benefit of working together. It is healthy and necessary that we all receive a reasonable reward for our contributions. We find ourselves in highly integrated and collaborative modern societies, many of which are very rich, so there cannot be any justification for large numbers of people being left poor.

Social engineering

The neoliberal era has seen the imposition of a doctrine that most social interactions can be replaced by market mechanisms. This has caused dramatic changes in our societies. There has been a rise in individuality, selfishness, insecurity, inequality, poverty, and our families, communities and social fabric have been weakened. Democracy has been weakened and often actively subverted by the wealthy. The rise in international hostility that has accompanied these changes has been used as an excuse to seriously diminish our legal and civil rights, and to increase the power of the rich and powerful.

This has been just as much an exercise in social engineering as socialism and communism. Elevating competition as the primary means of social organisation is as misguided as elevating cooperation as the primary means of social organisation. A healthy life is one that balances individuality and group needs, that balances competition and cooperation. This ought to be obvious in daily life, and it is an insight that goes back at least to Taoist wisdom from millennia ago.

It is instructive to think about how a healthy society that values its children might be different from the neoliberal vision. In *Children of the Lucky Country?*[63], the authors consider what qualities our societies might emphasise if they are to escape their present pathology. Top of their list are *equality* and *trust*.

These are followed by *more emphasis on collective gains* and *valuing parenting*. If we care about our future we must value our children, and if we value our children we must value parents. They observe that modern workplaces are so hostile to the needs of parents that many people who value their careers are having only one or no children, even though they might wish to combine their career with parenting.

Perhaps it is worth completing the authors' list. Valuing childhood for children, rather than for adults, in other words letting kids just play, undirected so their natural creativity can blossom. *Preventing,* rather than curing. Caring for and saving the natural environment for children's futures. Providing safe built environments (as Cat Stevens sang so poignantly in 1970, *Where do the children play?*). Balancing technologies for children, in other words making more effort to bring out the benefits and limit the harm of the modern technologies that are now a major part of childhood. Ensuring that we *all* care for children.

By focussing on the material, on money, on profit, we are undermining all of these qualities in our societies. When you focus on the effect on children, you see we are exploiting our own children, profiting in ways that are harmful to them. That is one of the main features of the grand social experiment being conducted by the neoliberal social engineers.

Political correctness

Anyone who uses or promotes expressions that attempt to be respectful to particular social groups, or that attempt to replace older discriminatory terms with more neutral terms, is likely to be derided by the right as *politically correct*. Examples would be saying "person of colour" instead of negro, "ethnic minority" instead of wog, or the clumsy "his or her" to avoid gender imbalance. The term implies, minimally, a rejection of the need for such nonsense, but it commonly also expresses a defensiveness, a sensitivity to being implicitly accused of being racist, sexist or whatever.

Right-wing usage also carries an implication that "the left" is following a doctrinaire socialist script. This has a historical basis, in that socialists did use the term, perhaps self-mockingly, to describe those who followed a party line too zealously. It is a small step then to the implication, in the minds of the right, that the politically correct are trying to restrict "freedom", the right of a neoliberal to do or say what he likes.

This is all very ironic, because neoliberals have systematically ridiculed, derided and attacked any criticism of their own program and world view. Any suggestion that markets are not perfect, that "intervention" in markets might be appropriate, that some people are acquiring too much wealth and power, that US foreign policy might be influenced by the greed of its dominant corporations, that global warming is caused by people, and so on, is likely to attract the ire of right-wing PC enforcers. The enforcers include politicians, radio shock jocks, media commentators, many reporters and editors more generally, intellectuals and the legions of anonymous, reactionary commenters on internet web sites.

The so-called political left that has survived beyond the 1970s has been thoroughly intimidated. Any questioning of large concentrations of wealth draws the charge "class warfare" and they run scuttling for cover. A favourite in Australia is that any questioning of the so-called "American alliance" (meaning obsequious fawning at the feet of the US political establishment) is attributed to "anti-American elements", and the Labor Party scuttles for cover.

200

The right-wing enforcement of their political correctness has been far more pervasive and vicious than anything attributed to poor old lefties. The Bush II administration was infamously vindictive towards anyone who questioned it. In Australia the Howard government became adept at the *dog whistle* – the coded statement that would bring out the attack-dog enforcers. Shredding of reputations, character assassination, threats of legal action or actual legal action, defamatory misrepresentations or outright lies are all used routinely.

Presumably this assault has been encouraged by the wimpishness of the "left" of the political mainstream, which lost its way amid the turmoil of the 1970s. I'm speaking of liberals in the US, Tony Blair's Labor in the UK, and Hawke-Keating Labor in Australia. Since then the "left" has been bullied, wedged, pushed and dragged ever further to the right, so that now they are well to the right of the center-right parties of the 1960s, while the right has become ever more extreme.

With a clear analysis of the fundamental flaws in the neoclassical-neoliberal world view, and with a clear direction towards a humane, sustainable, managed-market economy that transcends socialism and capitalism, the right-wing assaults can readily be deflect, or turned back upon them.

Class warfare

Any questioning of the desirability of large concentrations of wealth, or of the behaviour of the super-wealthy, is likely to be labelled class warfare. There has been such a successful denigration of all things egalitarian, over many decades, that very few seem to be willing to make the obvious riposte – who started it?

There would not be any communists or socialists if capitalists had not behaved so badly. There would not have been serfs, slaves or revolutionaries if kings, pharaohs and despots had not behaved so badly. There would be no classes if conquerors did not conquer. The English class system dates back a thousand years to the Norman conquest. The Indian caste system incorporates the repression of dark-skinned locals by Aryan conquerors.

The United States was founded in a Revolutionary War fought to free itself from the concentrated wealth and arbitrary power of the English monarchy. Yet the founding fathers and revolutionary soldiers have been twice betrayed.

During and after the US Civil War wealthy industrialists began to assemble vast empires that culminated in the *gilded age* of the late nineteenth century. Dramatically improved transport and communications, through railways and the telegraph, allowed capitalists to reach markets and assemble empires much larger than had been possible before, and the rise of new the technologies and industries allowed the operation of the coloniser effect, in which those entering early gain advantages. Over the same period explicit limitations on the charters of corporations, expressly intended to prevent money gaining power over people, were progressively removed by compliant legislators. This culminated in 1886 with the alleged decision of the US Supreme Court that corporations have the rights of natural persons. It is questioned whether the Court ever made such a decision, but the precedent quickly became entrenched anyway[83].

The gilded age is also known as the age of robber barons. A plutocracy took control of the US, controlled by a few hundred super-wealthy families, while the great majority was impoverished[59]. It is not unreasonable to characterise the claimed 1886 Supreme Court decision as a counter-revolution, and the end of the first United States republic.

There followed a long struggle to retrieve control from the plutocrats. The plutocratic excesses crashed the economy in 1929, but it was not until the emergency of World War II that legislators found enough spine, under heavy pressure from electors, to impose taxes at a level that clawed back some of the wealth and control for the common people[59]. Comparable developments in other industrial countries enabled the rise of the middle class in the post-war boom, a rise in the wealth of more people than the world had ever seen.

According to Pizzigati[59], plutocratic control of the US was essentially broken in the 1950s and 1960s, yet the McCarthyist witch hunts of the 1950s removed or intimidated those who championed the ordinary people, claiming that even moderate socialists provided cover for a communist takeover. Even the pragmatic arguments of the likes of Bowles[64] and Paul[65], that wealth must be more equitably shared if the appeal of communism was to be countered and the economy was to reach its potential, were not taken up by successor "liberals".

This political history is the other half of the story of the rise of the neoliberal ideology. A parallel push from economists championed the alleged merits of free markets, Hayek being a principal figure[84,85]. Hayek himself can only be called an extremist who believed that human empathy and cooperation were primitive characteristics that we would soon evolve beyond[85]. The free-market message of some schools of economics (Austrian and neoclassical in particular) were just what the embattled plutocrats wanted to hear: the best thing anyone can do is to make money as fast as they can. Free-market economists were showered with money, think tanks were established and

203

they quickly gained influence in "conservative" political circles.

The difficulties of the 1970s, including oil embargoes and inflation from the mis-managed US war effort in Vietnam, created the pretext for a plutocratic push-back that triumphed in 1979 and 1980 with the elections of Margaret Thatcher and Ronald Reagan. Taxes on the wealthy were quickly reduced and markets were deregulated, particularly financial markets. Since then the wealthy have captured most of the new wealth created in the US, and much of the wealth world wide. Super-fortunes now eclipse those of the gilded age, and the wealth of ordinary people has stagnated, and gone backwards since the GFC. Whole countries are now intimidated and pushed around by gigantic transnational corporations. The plutocracy is back.

The Bush II administration in the US was remarkable for the blatancy with which it challenged the founding principles of the US. The powerful know best, restraints on the exercise of power are to be broken or ignored, government, acting for the people, is to be drastically curtailed, and the role of government is to be restricted to defending the property rights of capitalists and to fighting wars. The Obama administration (with many plutocrat apologists in its ranks) is either complicit or oblivious to what is really happening.

The modern history of the United States[59] thus provides a lesson. The people rebelled against the arbitrary power of wealth, and gained a modicum of democratic power. Plutocrats gradually found new ways to gain influence, ultimately almost completely erasing the triumph of the US democratic republic. There followed a series of drastic crises. The First World War was triggered by national plutocratic rivalries. The Great Depression resulted from the speculative excesses of plutocrats with more money than they could usefully spend[59]. The Second World War resulted from mismanagement of the post-war settlement, the interwar German economy and the Depression. These crises eventually discredited the plutocrats sufficiently for their power finally to be reined in. However they pushed back again, in new ways, and have regained control.

Is it "class war" to argue against super-concentrations of wealth, and its associated political power? Is it class war to point out that plutocracy leads to political corruption, subversion of democracy, human rights abuses, and poor economic performance leading into economic collapse? Well if it is, then the plutocrats have created the class distinctions. Once again, if they did not behave so badly there would not be a building movement opposing them.

11

WELLBEING

Abject failure

THE purpose of an economy is to support the society it is part of. Supporting the society includes supporting every individual in the society, so at the very least they have *access* to a dignified livelihood. Dignity requires not being markedly lower in status than most people, and that includes not being markedly poorer. Wealthy countries can readily afford to ensure everyone lives at least a dignified and modestly comfortable life, substantially better than subsistence. It is probably within the means of most poorer countries to keep people from falling below subsistence and into poverty or starvation. It can be the intention of all humanity to help poorer countries find the way to raise all their people to modest physical sufficiency.

I contend that the above statements are just expressions of common human decency, and require no more justification than, for example, "We hold ... that all [people] are created equal".

Apologists for the present regime contend it is the best way to provide for all. Plutocrats contend simply that they are the ones who know best how to create wealth, but the evidence from the two modern eras of plutocracy contradicts their claim, and anyway extremes of wealth and poverty are not compatible with human dignity for everyone. Mainstream economists claim to have shown that free markets maximise wealth creation, but their theory is so deficient as to be a joke, and the same evidence is against them as well.

A more critical look at modern economies soon reveals reasons why wealth is very unevenly spread. For example, this book has identified a series of mechanisms that operate within our economies to transfer large amounts of wealth from the poor and middle class to the rich. The list here is a little longer than the first such list I compiled, in *Economia*[29], reflecting continuing analysis, in *The Nature of the Beast*[10] and here. At the conclusion of *Economia* I wrote

> These mechanisms are human creations. Since power within our human societies flows so readily from wealth, the lack of freedom of action and lifestyle that many suffer are, by implication, also due to these created economic mechanisms. ... In other words, our present economic mechanisms create a great deal of both poverty and oppression.
>
> From this perspective, I find the present condition of humanity to be deeply shocking. Our vaunted economic systems (and here I don't separate capitalism from communism or any other materialist-industrial *ism*) don't come even close to providing for the most basic needs of most of humanity. Their record is not one of mediocrity,

but of abject failure. They create human misery on a vast scale. They threaten humanity with decimation or extinction, either through the propensity of our present societies for violence or through our assaults on our own life support system.

Several aspects of mainstream economics feed this abject failure, other than its absurd theorising. It counts the wrong things, and counts them in a way that blithely counts the bad as good. It legitimises a monetary system grown rather directly from fraudulent practices of medieval money changers[71,75,76,80]. That monetary system pumps money to the wealthy, and operates at a fundamental level to destabilise the whole economy. Mainstream economics legitimises frenetic gambling in the financial markets that is parasitic and destabilising. It overlooks fundamental distinctions, such as that land is not a manufacturable commodity, and that a financial "asset" has no more substance than a promise. It neglects crucial factors, such as that some wealth is intrinsically collective, and the kinds of ownership we avail ourselves of play central roles in how wealth flows, and whether responsibility is evaded.

It has never been grasped within the mainstream that to be scientific requires something other than using mathematics. Mathematics is not even essential. What is essential is that the implications of a theory be compared with observations of the real world, to see if they provide useful guidance to the behaviour of the real world. Neoclassical economics is pseudo-science – it dresses itself up in the superficial garb of science, but it is not science.

In fact neoclassical economics is so far from being a useful first step towards creating a science that it is pre-scientific. It is not as useful as Ptolemy's description of the heavens, which gives moderately accurate predictions of the positions of the planets most of the time. Modern economies are clearly far from equilibrium all of the time, so a theory presuming equilibrium, or capable of depicting nothing other than near-equilibrium, is not a useful place to start. One has to look elsewhere for a toehold that can begin one's ascent to a vantage with a better view. In the meantime the neoclassical approach obstructs progress and seriously misleads and distorts society.

Begin again

We need to bypass mainstream economics and essentially start again. There is good understanding to be gained from modern systems theory and many other branches of modern knowledge. We know quite a lot about far-from-equilibrium, self-organising systems. Their detailed behaviour may not be predictable much of the time, but they have recognisable patterns of behaviour nevertheless. They have character. By studying that character we can learn to work with it and, ultimately, to guide it, the way sensitive people have learnt to work with horses, even wild horses.

With this kind of approach can hope to make economies humane and reasonably equitable. We can hope to have them nurture our planetary life support system instead of trashing it.

Foremost must be some choices. Do our economies exist to promote the growth of material consumption, and thus the consumption of the world on which we depend totally? Or do they exist to support the wellbeing of everyone? Do we include wellbeing in all its aspects: material, social, emotional and spiritual? Do we choose to manage economies so they provide reasonably for *everyone,* so that poverty is uncommon and dignity, respect and tolerance are widespread?

If we choose wellbeing for everyone, then we can start monitoring our wellbeing, as best we are able, qualitatively and quantitatively. We can abandon the pursuit of ever-increasing quantity, regardless of quality, through our present worship of GDP, the modern Mammon.

With a clear purpose and a sensible characterisation of our condition and progress, we can turn to actual management. Understanding of complexity, non-linearity and self-organisation within economies has already been advancing on the fringes of the mainstream. There are many useful studies leading to valuable insights, and a good survey is given by Beinhocker[26].

As well, many of the practical things we need to do, to live well while reducing our assault on the Earth, are already being done, but only on small scales. However the dominant paradigm undermines and derails them, preventing their widespread adoption. An important part of our challenge is to identify economic mechanisms that impede the good things, and to modify those mechanisms so they are supportive.

Similarly we can identify economic mechanisms that presently prevent or disrupt an equitable, just and sustainable society, and seek to modify or replace them with mechanisms that promote the welfare of our people and our social structure. The economy can be returned to its proper place, serving society not dictating to society.

In other words, markets can be a positive force, used wisely and appropriately. They are powerful, and properly tamed, managed and harnessed they might help us to improve our world faster than we presently dare to imagine.

Harnessing the wild horses

Beyond these generalities, some particular economic reforms have been identified in the course of this book. They have been discussed in more detail elsewhere[10,29], so only some signposts will be given here. The main purpose of this book is just to break through the mainstream wall of silence, to open the space for us to sensibly explore and debate our options.

Sensible measures of our wellbeing can be adopted immediately. They will never be perfect, so they ought and can to be refined as we go along. Not all of them need be quantitative either, other than for example polling people on their subjective evaluation of their own wellbeing. It is better to be heading roughly in the right direction than directly toward the precipice, which is where reliance on the GDP is taking us. GDP should be retired forthwith as a primary indicator. It may have been of some use to monitor levels of wartime production, but it profoundly distorts our priorities now.

Financial markets need to be restrained and returned to their proper place, which is to be a small segment of the economy that serves the needs of the productive economy. A primary device is the transaction tax, which should be just large enough to take most of the profit out of speculative games. That would reduce market turnover by a factor of 50 or more, dramatically reduce instability, prevent large amounts of wealth being stolen from those who helped to create it, and return control of our society to the political system.

There are a great many perverse subsidies that promote harmful activities, or activities that enrich a few at the expense of everyone else[82]. Examples are continuing large subsidies of fossil fuel extraction and use. In Australia these have been estimated to be on the order of $A10 billion per year, for a population 1/15th the US population[86]. That dwarfs the support given to energy efficiency and clean energy. Harmful subsidies will only be eliminated through political action. They are really symptoms of the corruption of our democracies at the systemic level.

There are many perverse incentives, due more to inattention or lack of imagination than to corruption. Typically, resource suppliers encourage us to use more, because their profits rise in simple proportion to throughput. Electricity suppliers, for example, could be paid for helping us to use less, it was done in California for a while[87], before the market fundamentalists encouraged Enron to wreck everything[88].

A powerful example has been set by billion-dollar carpet manufacturer Interface[89]. Instead of just selling carpet, they offered a floor covering service, including maintenance. At a stroke they reversed their incentive from maximising throughput to minimising it. They have made their carpet more durable, and recyclable. They have also eliminated most harmful substances. Their founder, the late Ray C. Anderson, set the company on a course to become the first "restorative" company – a company that actually improves the Earth as it does its business. They are not there yet, but they have come a long way.

Interface is only one of many exciting and inspiring stories of how, when we set our minds to it, we can create practical ways to live well while the Earth thrives around us.

We can be more adventurous in our use of alternative ownership models. In our societies the kind of ownership used is a major control on how both wealth and responsibility flow to all who are involved in an enterprise. Employee ownership removes the source of the main conflicts of the disastrous twentieth century, the conflicting wants of bosses and workers.

Two less familiar but profound reforms also await our attention. The first is to recognise what I have called *emergent community wealth,* the wealth that accrues to everyone in a community because of mutual proximity. It is the reason why land in city centers is more expensive than land on the outskirts, whether for business or residence. With appropriate ownership structures and careful management, that wealth can be retained for the benefit of the community instead of being captured as unearned windfalls by land speculators[44]. A major source of wealth inequality would thereby be removed.

The final reform is to the monetary and investment systems. The productive economy will be hostage to the vagaries of financial markets and risky investments so long as money continues to be supplied through bank "loans". It is high folly to allow the supply of our medium of exchange to depend on a mechanism at once so erratic and so vulnerable to manipulation.

Money can be supplied independently of the loans and investment process, simply by providing everyone with demand accounts somewhat similar to a line of credit or a credit card. As explained in Chapter 9 a fee structure can be adopted that encourages rapid circulation of money, and thereby minimises the debt that is intrinsic to token money.

The change that would depart most from current business doctrines and practice is to cease using new money for investment. Only then would the money supply to Main Street be stabilised, and a major cause of recessions and depressions removed. Investment would come instead from savings, wealth already accrued. Instead of borrowing from the future, from our children, we would then be accumulating from the past. We would pass on a gift of productivity to our children, instead of the burden of debt and risk.

This last change may generate reflexive opposition from the financial and banking sectors, but investment would not be so different once the transition was made. However the reward to the whole of society makes it clear we need to do it. The reform would remove the major source of debt, the major source of instability driving booms, busts, recessions and depressions, and what is currently perhaps the major flow of unearned wealth to the wealthy.

Economies that serve and nurture

The goal and effect of these changes would be nothing more, or less, than to get markets working they way they are supposed to work. Markets indeed are powerful. Much of that power comes from the way they facilitate the evaluation of a vast amount of information. The evaluation is not necessarily "rational", as neoclassical economists pretend, but it is far more effective than a bureaucracy could be, because it is distributed among all market participants. Hayek was correct in recognising this power of markets[85]. However he and the neoclassical economists were quite incorrect in claiming that *free* markets will deliver desirable results efficiently.

At present our market systems are close to anarchical. In some contexts the invisible hand operates and delivers a good result. In others the invisible foot operates and delivers a perverse result. In yet other contexts, markets are manipulated for the benefit of a few. We might call this the operation of the *grasping hand.*

By divesting ourselves of the neoclassical myth, that free markets efficiently deliver desirable results, we remove the scales from our eyes. It is then not so difficult to see how the incentives under which a market segment operates might be adjusted so it delivers what we want. A few examples have been mentioned above, and earlier in this book.

The result, at a minimum, ought to be wellbeing delivered more efficiently to greater numbers, because the

215

delivery would be effected by the markets themselves, rather than retro-actively by clumsy government programs that only partially compensate for market malfunctions. Thus government could be reduced, as neoliberals so fervently desire – but not eliminated. Social welfare ought also to improve, as socialists have fervently desired, but through an alternative approach.

Beyond that economic result, it will become possible to restore economies to their proper place, which is to support the kind of society we wish to live in. A less unequal society will be to everyone's benefit, even the plutocrats who temporarily live so high at everyone else's expense but who undermine the basis of their own wealth and wellbeing.

It will also become possible to restore our economies and societies to their appropriate place in the natural world. Fundamentally that means we must acknowledge we are inextricably and intimately a part of the living world around us. All the food we eat, all the water we drink, all the air we breathe exists and is purified by its cycling through the living world around us. The health of the biosphere is our health, and as it dies we die. We must learn to live again as part of the miraculous living world around us, if we wish for our children and their children to have an indefinite future on this amazing planet.

At present social and environmental needs are quite secondary to the alleged needs of our pathological economic system. The quality of our communities and larger social fabric is only addressed after "the economy" is attended to, and commonly the economy has damaged our society more than the bandaid retro-active actions can hope to rectify.

In the sane society we might have, if we can abandon the present pathology, there will be no conflict between "the economy" and "social welfare", nor between "the economy" and "the environment". Rather, the central purpose of the economy will be to support society, including its natural life support system. There may be trade-offs to be made, but they will be made within the economic process, and not left to be ineffectually attended to after the economy has further damaged our lives and our home.

To a socialist (and there are still a few left in the world), my proposed reliance on markets might seem to be anathema. Given how dysfunctional markets have been, that is understandable. I do not imagine the task is small, nor that we can thoroughly transform our economies in any short time. However I would expect improvements to become apparent rather quickly as we attend to some of the major dysfunctions. If the socialist goals of social and economic justice begin to be achieved by means other than pervasive government ownership and management then perhaps socialists will begin to see the benefit of sensibly managing markets.

To a traditional conservative (as distinct from the radical-right neoliberals), my proposal to manage the incentives under which markets operate may still seem intrusive on the rights of individuals to pursue their own destiny. However if we are to live in any kind of society at all (and not as dispersed and isolated family groups, which never was how human beings live and is anyway now impossible), there is always a concession of some personal autonomy to the good of the group. The philosopher Karl Popper has argued, soundly I think, that individual autonomy is maximised not by zero law, but by an optimum amount of law[90]. Zero law, true anarchy, merely leaves the field open to bullies and warlords, who will quickly reduce our autonomy to little or nothing. I would argue that our goal can be just such an *optimum* amount of management, and that our personal autonomy would be greater than in the present regime, which features both intrusive government rules and intrusive corporate practices.

To anyone encountering these ideas for the first time, they may seem Utopian. I am very clear that treating some of our current ailments will not yield some idyllic existence free of all conflict and want. We will still have conflicting interests. We will still squabble. However we may hope to avoid the monumental disasters of the twentieth century, and the catastrophe that looms if we do not soon stop fouling the planet. With an increasingly more visible prospect that everyone on the planet might gain access to a dignified and sufficient livelihood, then perhaps we will be less ready to resort to violence and war. We will not have to do particularly well to do better than we did this past century. That will still be a long way short of Utopia.

Others may prefer the term *idealist*. Again, this is not about perfection. Plato thought in terms of the *ideal*, the perfect, but I do not. There is no such thing as perfection in nature, indeed the concept makes no sense. Every living organism, including ourselves, is scrambling to maintain a place amidst the continually shuffling and changing order of creatures and conditions around us.

Plato thought there was a conceptual *ideal horse*, and that all real horses are imperfect approximations. That is such a negative conception of the magnificence of a horse. Descartes applied the same thinking to people, that we can exist as pure minds but we live in imperfect, *corrupt* bodies. No, the horse was excellent at what it was, good enough to survive and persist on the Asian steppes, or in the stables of rich humans. People have been excellent at what we are, versatile, innovative and cooperative enough to survive and persist on the dangerous African savannah. If we are wise, as distinct from perfect, we will find the ways to persist for some time yet, while manifesting our own magnificence.

The term idealist also implies simply someone with ideas so impractical they are never likely to be realised. There are three responses to the fatalist attitude that dismisses new ideas. If we don't take the trouble to imagine better ways, we will certainly be trapped in our current predicament. If we all agree it can't be done, we will certainly be correct. If we don't change our ways, and soon, the Earth will change them for us.

Recent history demonstrates that change can come quickly, once enough people realise it is possible. Few people outside East Germany foresaw the collapse of the communist regime and the tearing down of the Berlin Wall. The regime had been losing legitimacy in the minds of the people for a long time. The critical point, the tipping point, came when enough people put their heads up, and they realised how many they were, and therefore how powerful. There was not even a fight, the regime just whimpered and departed.

We don't have to put up with the superficial farce that our politics have become. We *can* talk about the important issues. We *can* expect to be told the truth. We *can* contemplate the displacement of the present, corrupted political parties. We *can* expect healthy food, a decent income, a healthy neighbourhood. We *can* expect the world to be getting better, not worse. *Yes we can.* And we can expect action, not just fine words.

If we stop those who exploit and violate other people in our name, we need *no longer* be threatened by terrorism or war. Fundamentally, we stop them by withholding or withdrawing our approval of them. In a dictatorship that is not so easy, but in a democracy it means we must change the way we vote.

Most of us, already, do not want things to continue as they are. Most of us recognise that we must change the way we live if we are to leave plentiful opportunity and a rich planet for our children[91], but we are afraid to say so. We just need to discover how many we are, and how powerful.

If, then, we realise markets can be harnessed to support the goals of everybody's individual wellbeing, a healthy society and a healthy natural world, we may discover we can improve our condition much more rapidly and completely than we could have imagined, immersed as we are in the current pathology.

Rediscovering our place

We are so immersed in our daily lives and in the usual world around us it is hard to step back and gain some perspective on our current condition. One way we might do that is to listen to those who have never joined in the obsessions of the modern industrial, material way of life. We can remind ourselves that many societies have lived by quite different values. Even Western society, six centuries ago, was dominated by a quite different perception of the world and our place in it. Further afield, there have been many societies, large and small, that have lived by many world views.

The Kogi, Wiwa and Arhuaco people live near the northern extremity of South America, in the Sierra Nevada de Santa Marta of Colombia, an uplift close to the coast and separate from the Andes[92]. These people are the descendants of the Tairona civilisation, which fought the Spanish conquerors and were not entirely vanquished.

220

The survivors retreated to the mountains with their own culture uncontaminated by Spanish Christianity. They vowed to stop fighting and follow peaceful ways. Their culture preserves the intimate physical and spiritual interdependence of the people and the landscape. They regard themselves as the Elder Brothers, the ones who remember how one must live with the Earth. They view with dismay and horror the folly of the Younger Brothers, who have forgotten the ways and resist relearning them.

Having survived and thrived for hundreds of years in their mountain home, they are now being directly affected by the folly of the Younger Brothers. The glaciers and snows of their mountains are shrinking alarmingly, as are mountain glaciers all over the world. Bands of leftist and rightist fighters invade, to grow the lucrative coca, and the army pursues them. Many of the people have been killed by these intruders, though they refuse to give up their peaceful ways: "The spiritual world and the world of guns do not go together". "The ancestors say that one day the Younger Brother will wake up. But only when the violence of nature is on top of him."

In 2004 these people issued a joint declaration:

"Who will pay the universal mother for the air we breath, the water that flows, the light of the sun? Everything that exists has a spirit that is sacred and must be respected. Our law is the law of origins, the law of life. We invite all the Younger Brothers to be guardians of life. We affirm our promise to the Mother, and issue a call for solidarity and unity for all peoples and all nations."

AFTERWORD

This book has indicated how we may create fairer, more stable and more enduring economies, but it has not gone very far beyond economics in discussing how we may better live together on our only home planet. However a great deal is already happening. Mostly it is at the small scale, but a major goal of economic reforms will be to ensure economic mechanisms promote these other reforms, rather than hindering them as at present.

There are many groups cultivating local community and saner economic relationships at the small scale. There is a great deal being done to improve the efficiency with which we use Earth's precious resources. In fact the potential, and long-term, requirement is that we live like all other organisms, recycling all materials, producing no persistent toxins, and living off natural flows of energy, all the while maintaining a high quality of life. Some further sources follow.

One of the best is Gar Alperovitz' *What Then Must We Do*[45], which is very complementary to this book. He outlines many efforts at enterprise, community, city and state level to develop better economic processes, a key feature being "the democratisation of wealth" – in other words spreading ownership around. As importantly, he looks forward to how these many efforts might come together, and what strategies can help to bring that about. He sees that as successes build we not only learn better economic strategies but we build political constituencies with new visions of what is possible. The examples are all from the US, which will be of direct relevance for US readers. However it's well worth reading for non-US readers, because the examples are still very instructive and because it gives a concise sketch of how dysfunctional the United States is becoming under its extreme version of mainstream free-market fundamentalism. There, but for such good sense as we still retain, go we.

Community-Wealth.Org[93] is a comprehensive clearing house and promoter of the many activities, and many kinds of activities, in the United States to revive local communities by preserving and building their wealth under local ownership. A close complement to Alperovitz' book.

In Britain the *New Economics Foundation*[94] promotes innovative community and national-level initiatives, from preserving shopping streets against the predations of big-box stores and promoting transition towns to reforming the banking industry.

The supply of money to communities and beyond by now has a significant literature. Thomas Greco's *The End of Money and the Future of Civilization*[76] covers the topic in some depth, though his earlier *New Money for Healthy Communities*[73] more directly addresses community-level money. Deirdre Kent's *Healthy Money, Healthy Planet*[95] covers the topic in the New Zealand context.

The reform of energy and resource systems is not much covered in this book, but it is an important complement to the imperative to disperse and localise ownership, because many of the best resource options also involve distributed and local systems, including high efficiency and comprehensive recycling. The *Rocky Mountain Institute*[96] has long been a source of information and creative approaches. The book

Reinventing Fire[97] is an excellent compilation of energy options and illustration of their general approach.

My earlier books give more detail on many topics. *The Nature of the Beast*[10] is closer to this book, though giving more detail on the the ways we can reform market mechanisms, and the importance of social interactions. *Economia*[29] is a little dated in some of its economic arguments, especially on money, but it gives a very broad survey of the nature of the living world and our place in it, as a complement to exploring economies that can operate on the same principles, and therefore have the living world thrive around us. It also surveys energy and resource efficiency more comprehensively.

BIBLIOGRAPHY

1 Ormerod, P., *The Death of Economics*. 1994, London: Faber and Faber.

2 Keen, S., *Debunking Economics: the Naked Emperor of the Social Sciences*. 2001, Annandale (NSW), London, New York: Pluto Press, Zed Books, St. Martin's Press.

3 Keen, S., *Debunking Economics: The Naked Emperor Dethroned?* Second, revised and expanded ed. 2011: Zed Books.

4 Quiggin, J., *Zombie Economics: How Dead Ideas Still Walk among Us*. 2010, Princeton: Princeton University Press.

5 Galbraith, J.K., Some economists got it right. *Twill*, 2011. Vol. (14), doi: http://www.twill.info/issues/twill-14/index.html.

6 Sraffa, P., The law of returns under competitive conditions. *Economic Journal*, 1926. **40:** p. 538-550.

7 Keynes, J.M., *General Theory of Employment, Interest and Money*. 1936, London: Macmillan.

8 Minsky, H., The financial instability hypothesis: an interpretation of Keynes and an alternative to "standard" theory. *Nebraska Journal of Economics and Business*, 1977.

9 Baker, D., The folly of DC's desperate deficit fearmongers. *The Guardian*, 2013. Vol., doi: http://www.guardian.co.uk/commentisfree/2013/jan/28/folly-dc-deficit-fear-mongers.

10 Davies, G.F., *The Nature of the Beast: how economists mistook wild horses for a rocking chair.* 2012: Electronic copy available from http://betternature.wordpress.com/. 233 pp.

11 Heilbroner, R. and L. Thurow, *Economics Explained.* 1994, New York: Simon and Schuster.

12 Keen, S., Australian Debt Update. 2011. Vol., doi: http://www.debtdeflation.com/ blogs/2011/03/03/australian-debt-update/.

13 Wikipedia, National debt of the United States. 2013. Vol., doi: http://en.wikipedia.org/wiki/National_debt_of_the_United_States.

14 Wikipedia, Australian national debt. 2013. Vol., doi: http://en.wikipedia.org/wiki/ Australian_national_debt.

15 Austin, A., Debt and deficit Downunder — don't be so damned depressed! *Independent Australia,* 2013. Vol., doi: http://www.independentaustralia.net/2013/ politics/debt-and-deficit-downunder-dont-be-so-damned-depressed/?utm_medium=email&utm_campaign=IA+Newsletter%3A+Our+Samizdat+Years&utm_source=YMLP&utm_term=Read+the+st...

16 Morgenson, G. and M.M. Weinstein, *Teachings of two nobelists also proved their undoing,* in *New York Times.* 1998.

17 Taleb, N.N., *The Black Swan.* Second ed. 2010: Random House. 480 pp.

18 RWER. *Keen, Roubini and Baker win Revere Award for Economics,* 2010. Real World Economics Review Blog. http://rwer.wordpress.com/2010/05/13/keen-roubini-and-baker-win-revere-award-for-economics-2/.

19 Schlefer, J., *Today's most michievous misquotation,* in *The Atlantic Monthly.* 1998. p. March, http://www.theatlantic.com/past/docs/issues/98mar/misquote.htm;

Buckley, I. *Learning from Adam Smith - help at hand today,* 2009. The British Empire, http://www.britishempire.

co.uk/index.php. http://www.britishempire.co.uk/article/adamsmith.htm, or http://users.cyberone.com.au/ibuckley/AdamSmith_Essay.pdf (pdf 418 kb);

Meeropol, M., Another Distortion of Adam Smith: The Case of the "Invisible Hand". 2004. Vol. **Working Paper 79**, doi: http://www.peri.umass.edu/fileadmin/pdf/working_papers/working_papers_51-100/WP79.pdf; P e r s k y, J., Retrospectives: Adam Smith's Invisible Hands. *Journal of Economics Perspectives,* 1989(4): p. 195-201.

20 Colombo, J., Black Monday – the Stock Market Crash of 1987. *Stock Market Crash!,* 2013. Vol., doi: http://www.stock-market-crash.net/1987-crash/.

21 Eggertsson, G.B. and P. Krugman, Debt, Deleveraging, and the Liquidity Trap: A Fisher-Minsky-Koo Approach. *Quarterly Journal of Economics,* 2012. **127:** p. 1469-1513.

22 Keen, S., A monetary Minsky model of the Great Moderation and the Great Recession. *Journal of Economic Behavior & Organization,* 2012. **86:** p. 221-235.

23 Toohey, B., *Tumbling Dice.* 1994, Melbourne: William Heinemann Australia. 348 pp.

24 Rothschild, M., *Bionomics: Economy as Ecosystem.* 1990, New York: Henry Holt. 423 pp.

25 Greider, W., *One World, Ready or Not.* 1997: Simon and Schuster.

26 Beinhocker, E.D., *The Origin of Wealth.* 2006, Boston: Harvard Business School Press.

27 Prigogine, I. and I. Stengers, *Order Out of Chaos.* 1984, New York: Bantam.

28 Waldrop, M.M., *Complexity.* 1992, New York: Touchstone. 380 pp.

29 Davies, G.F., *Economia: New Economic Systems to Empower People and Support the Living World.* 2004, Sydney: ABC

Books. Electronic copy available at http://betternature. wordpress.com/.

30 Daly, H.E. and J.B. Cobb Jr., *For the Common Good.* 2nd ed. 1994, Boston: Beacon.

31 Hamilton, C. and H. Saddler, *The Genuine Progress Indicator.* Discussion Paper 14, 1997, The Australia Institute: Canberra.

32 Hamilton, C. and R. Denniss, *Tracking well-being in Australia – the Genuine Progress Indicator 2000.* Discussion Paper 35, 2000, The Australia Institute, www.tai.org.au: Canberra.

33 Waring, M., *If Women Counted.* 1988, San Francisco: Harper & Row.

34 Cobb, C., M. Glickman, and C. Cheslog, *The Genuine Progress Indicator, 2000 Update.* 2001, Redefining Progress, www. redefiningprogress.org: Oakland, CA.

35 Hamilton, C. and E. Mail, *Downshifting in Australia: a sea-change in the pursuit of happiness.* Discussion Paper 50, 2003, Australia Institute: Canberra.

36 Hamilton, C., *Downshifting in Britain: a sea-change in the pursuit of happiness.* Discussion Paper 58, 2003, Australia Institute: Canberra.

37 Berg, A.G. and J.D. Ostry, Equality and efficiency. *Finance and Development,* 2011. **48**(3): p. 12-15.

38 Reich, R.B., *The Limping Middle Class,* in *New York Times.* 2011: New York, NY.

39 Grille, R., *Parenting for a Peaceful World.* 2008, Richmond, UK: The Children's Project.

40 Kurtzman, J., *The Death of Money.* 1993, New York: Simon and Shuster.

41 Smith, K., A. Ozimek, and N. Blanchard. *Economic update slides,* 2011. Modeled Behavior. http://modeledbehavior. com/2011/07/17/economic-update-slides/.

42 Keen, S., *Deeper in Debt.* 2007, Centre for Policy Development, http://www.cpd.org.au.

43 George, H. and B. Drake, *Progress and Poverty.* 1879/2006: Robert Schalkenbach Foundation.

44 Turnbull, S., *A framework for designing sustainable urban communities.* 2007, International Institute for Self Governance.

45 Alperovitz, G., *What Then Must We Do?: Straight Talk about the Next American Revolution.* 2013: Chelsea Green Publishing.

46 Foley, L., Canberra's Leasehold Land System. 2008. Vol., doi: http://www.prosper.org.au/2008/01/16/canberra/; Brennan, F., *Canberra in Crisis.* 1971, Canberra: Dalton Publishing Company.

47 Mondragon, Mondragon Corporation (Wikipedia). Vol., doi: http://en.wikipedia.org/wiki/Mondragon_Corporation; Mondragon. *Mondragón Corporación Cooperativa.* http://www.mondragon-corporation.com/ENG.aspx.

48 Schumacher, E.F., *Small is Beautiful.* 1974, London: Abacus.

49 Bader, S. *Scott Bader – Multinational Chemical Company.* http://www.scottbader.com/.

50 Gates, J.R., *The Ownership Solution.* 1998, Reading, MA: Addison-Wesley.

51 Garofalo, P., The Walmart heirs have the same net worth and the bottom 30 percent of Americans. *Think Progress* http://thinkprogress.org/, 2011. Vol., doi: http://thinkprogress.org/economy/2011/12/09/385941/walmart-heirs-worth-30-percent-bottom/?mobile=nc.

52 Quinn, D., *Ishmael.* 1995: Bantam.

53 Quinn, D., *Beyond Civilization: Humanity's Next Great Adventure.* 1999, New York: Three Rivers Press.

54 Basque, Basque people (Wikipedia). Vol., doi: https://en.wikipedia.org/wiki/Basque_people.

55 Turnbull, S., *A New Way to Govern: Organisations and Society After Enron. NEF Pocketbooks*, ed. D. Nicholson-Lord. Vol. **6**. 2002, London: New Economics Foundation, www.neweconomics.org.

56 Buck, J. and S. Villines, *We The People: Consenting to a Deeper Democracy*. 2007, Washington D.C.: Sociocracy.info. 277 pp; Sociocracy, Sociocracy (Wikipedia). Vol., doi: http://en.wikipedia.org/wiki/Sociocracy.

57 Bell, S., *Ungoverning the Economy*. 1997, Melbourne: Oxford University Press. 324 pp.

58 Kervick, D., Market Myths and the Real Drivers of American Progress. *Rugged Egalitarianism*, http://ruggedegalitarianism.wordpress.com, 2013. Vol., doi: http://ruggedegalitarianism.wordpress.com/2013/10/20/market-myths-and-the-real- drivers-of-american-progress/.

59 Pizzigati, S., *The Rich Don't Always Win: The Forgotten Triumph over Plutocracy that Created the American Middle Class, 1900-1970*. 2013: Seven Stories Press.

60 Weisbrot, M., D. Baker, and D. Rosnick, *The Scorecard on Development: 25 Years of Diminished Progress*. 2005, Center for Economic and Policy Research, www.cepr.net/ index. html: Washington D. C.

61 Mishel, L., Top group takes large slice of income growth. *Economic Policy Institute, http://www.epi.org/economic_snapshots/entry/top_incomes_grow_while_bottom_incomes_stagnate/*, 2010. Posted.

62 Wilkinson, R. and K. Pickett, *The Spirit Level: Why Equality is Better for Everyone*. 2011: Bloomsbury Press.

63 Stanley, F., S. Richardson, and M. Prior, *Children of the Lucky Country? How Australian society has turned its back on children, and why they matter*. 2005, Sydney: Pan Macmillan Australia.

64 Bowles, C., *Tomorrow Without Fear*. 1946, New York: Simon and Schuster.

65 Paul, R., *Taxation for Prosperity*. 1947/2012: Literary Licensing.

66 Adler, M., *Economics for the Rest of Us: Debunking the Science that Makes Life Dismal*. 2009: New Press. 224 pp.

67 Dugger, W.M., *Corporate Hegemony*. 1989, New York: Greenwood Press.

68 Millward, R., *State enterprise in Britain in the twentieth century*, in The Rise and Fall of State-Owned Enterprise in the Western World, P.A. Toninelli, Editor. 2000, Cambridge University Press: Cambridge, UK. p. 157-84.

69 Mishel, L. *The State of Working America*. http://stateofworkingamerica.org/.

70 Riegel, E.C., *Flight From Inflation*. 1978, Los Angeles: The Heather Foundation, Box 48, San Pedro, CA 90773.

71 Lietaer, B., *The Future of Money*. 2001, London: Century.

72 Gessell, S., *The Natural Economic Order*. 1934, San Antonio, TX: The Free Economy Publishing Co. (Translated from the sixth German edition of Die Natürliche Wirtschaftsordnung, Rudolf Zitzmann Verlag, Berlin, 1904.).

73 Greco, T.H., Jr., *New Money for Healthy Communities*. 1994, Tucson, AZ: Thomas H. Greco, Jr., P.O. Box 42663, Tucson AZ 85733.

74 Fisher, I., *Stamp Scrip*. 1933, New York: Adelphi Company.

75 Kennedy, M., *Interest and Inflation Free Money*. 1988, Steyerberg: Permakulture Institut e.V., Ginsterweg 5, D-3074 Steyerberg, Germany.

76 Greco, T.H., Jr., *The End of Money and the Future of Civilization*. 2009, White River Junction, VT: Chelsea Green.

77 Goodwin, J., *Greenback: the almighty dollar and the invention of America*. 2003: Penguin.

78 New_Economic_Perspectives. *New Economic Perspectives blog,* 2013. http://neweconomicperspectives.org/.

79 Wray, L.R., *Modern Money Theory: A Primer on Macroeconomics for Sovereign Monetary Systems.* 2012: Palgrave Macmillan.

80 Rowbotham, M., *The Grip of Death.* 1998, Charlbury, Oxfordshire: Jon Carpenter Publishing.

81 Bornstein, D., *The Price of a Dream.* 1996, Dhaka, Bangladesh: The University Press. 370 pp.

82 Myers, N., *Perverse Subsidies: How Misused Tax Dollars Harm the Environment and the Economy.* 2001, Covelo, CA: Island Press.

83 Hartmann, T., *Unequal Protection: the rise of corporate dominance and the theft of human rights.* 2002: Rodale Books.

84 Hayek, F.A., *The Fatal Conceit: The Errors of Socialism. Collected Works of FA Hayek,* ed. W. Bartley. Vol. **1**. 1998, Chicago: University of Chicago Press.

85 McKnight, D., *Beyond Right and Left.* 2005, Sydney: Allen & Unwin. 298 pp.

86 Henry, D. *Australia spends $11 billion more encouraging pollution than cleaning it up,* 2011. Australian Conservation Foundation. http://www.acfonline.org.au/articles/news.asp?news_id=3308&eid=11731.

87 von Weizsäcker, E., A.B. Lovins, and L.H. Lovins, *Factor Four: Doubling Wealth, Halving Resource Use.* 1997, St. Leonards: Allen & Unwin.

88 Slocum, T., Behind the blackouts. *TomPaine.com,* 2006. Vol., doi: http://www.tompaine.com/articles/2006/07/28/behind_the_blackouts.php.

89 Anderson, R.C., *Business Lessons from a Radical Industrialist.* 2010, New York: St. Martins Press.

90 Magee, B., *Popper. Modern Masters.* 1973: Fontana. 109 pp; Popper, K., *The Open Society and It's Enemies.* 2002: Routledge.

91 Ray, P.H. and S.R. Anderson, *The Cultural Creatives*. 2000, New York: Harmony Books.

92 Davis, W., *The Wayfinders*. 2009, Perth: University of Western Australia Press.

93 Community-Wealth.Org. *Community-Wealth.Org*. http:// community-wealth.org/.

94 New_Economics_Foundation. *New Economics Foundation*. http://www.neweconomics.org/.

95 Kent, D., *Healthy Money, Healthy Planet*. 2005, Nelson, NZ: Craig Potton Publishing.

96 Rocky. *Rocky Mountain Institute*. www.rmi.org.

97 Lovins, A.B., *Reinventing Fire*. 2011, White River Junction, VT: Chelsea Green Publishing.

ABOUT THE AUTHOR

Dr. Geoff Davies is a retired Senior Fellow (now a Visiting Fellow) in geophysics at the Australian National University, http://people.rses.anu.edu.au/davies_g/. He blogs at http://betternature.wordpress.com/.

He is the author of *Economia: New economic systems to Empower People and Support the Living World* (ABC Books, Sydney, 2004), and the eBook *The Nature of the Beast: How economists mistook wild horses for a rocking chair.*

He has authored over one hundred scientific papers and two scientific books and has a Hirsch index of 38 (38 papers each with at least 38 citations, indicating significant international standing and influence).

In 2005 he was awarded the inaugural Augustus Love medal for geodynamics by the European Geosciences Union. He was selected in 1992 as a Fellow of the American Geophysical Union.

His most recent scientific book, *Mantle Convection for Geologists* (Cambridge University Press, 2011), won the 2011 Mary B. Ansari Best Reference Work Award of the GeoScience Information Society.

In economics he has also published two papers and several discussions on the blog site of the World Economics Association.

Books

Dynamic Earth: Plates, Plumes and Mantle Convection, Cambridge University Press, Cambridge, 1999.

Economia: New economic systems to Empower People and Support the Living World, ABC Books, Sydney, 2004.

Mantle Convection for Geologists, Cambridge University Press, Cambridge, 2011.

The Nature of the Beast: How Economists Mistook Wild Horses for a Rocking Chair, eBook 2012.

Economics papers

The Value of Simple Models, with Examples of Economic Dynamics, *real-world economics review,* no. 57, 2011, pp. 106-114, http://www.paecon.net/PAEReview/issue57/Davies57.pdf.

Bad theory, bad practice: bad ethics, *Economics in Society: The Ethical Dimension* online conference of the Real World Economics Association, 2012 Paper 16.

CPSIA information can be obtained at www.ICGtesting.com
Printed in the USA
LVOW12s1928070714

393231LV00009B/588/P

9 780992 360368